Autism Spectrum, Creativity and Emotions:

A New Point of View through Camila Falchi's Work

Elisabete Castelon Konkiewitz
Edward Benjamin Ziff

2018

English edition in United States of America

ISBN-13: 978-0692052716 (Pulso Editorial)
ISBN: 0692052716

Pulso Editorial, São José dos Campos , SP, Brazil
Autism Spectrum, Creativity and Emotions: a new point of view through Camila Falchi's work.
Elisabete Castelon Konkiewitz and Edward Benjamin Ziff

Layout and cover: Alexandre Marinho Vicente
Cover figure: Camila Falchi Parra Carvalho Silva

Printed in USA, 2018

This book has also been published in a Portuguese edition

Edition in Portuguese in October, 2017 – Brazil

Espectro do Autismo, Criatividade e Emoções : talentos e oportunidades criativas. Um novo olhar sobre o Espectro do Autismo através da obra de Camila Falchi. Autores: Elisabete Castelon Konkiewitz e Edward Benjamin Ziff -- São José dos Campos, SP : Pulso Editorial, 2017.

Avenida Anchieta, 885 (Jardim Nova América) São José dos Campos – SP –Brasil
CEP 12242-280 - Telefone/Fax: (12) 3942-1302
e-mail: atendimento@pulsoeditorial.com.br | *home-page*: http://www.pulsoeditorial.com.br

Impresso no Brasil/*Printed in Brazil*, com depósito legal na Biblioteca Nacional
conforme Decreto no. 1.825, de 20 de dezembro de 1907.

ISBN: 978-858298086
Editor responsável: Vicente José Assencio Ferreira
Diagramação e capa: Alexandre Marinho Vicente
Figura da capa: Camila Falchi Parra Carvalho Silva

About the authors

Elisabete Castelon Konkiewitz received a medical degree from UNIFESP (São Paulo Federal University) in 1993 and a doctorate in Neurology from the German university Technische Universität München, in 2002. She received the title of specialist in Neurology from the Brazilian Academy of Neurology and the title of specialist in Psychiatry from the Brazilian Association of Psychiatry. Since 2008, she has been an associate professor at the Federal University of Grande Dourados (UFGD) in Central West Brazil, where she lectures on neurology, psychiatry and neurobiology and supervises public clinics for Parkinson's disease and for people living with HIV infection. She attends patients with neurologic and psychiatric diseases at her medical practice in Dourados. She has written books and scientific articles in the areas of neuroscience, learning and education, including her book together with Angela Virgolim, "Altas Habilidades/Superdotação, Inteligência e Criatividade – Uma Visão Multidisciplinar" (High Abilities/Giftedness, Intelligence and Creativity - A Multidisciplinary Vision), which was awarded the prestigious Brazilian Jabuti Prize (Prêmio Jabuti) in 2015 in the area of Education. Dr. Castelon Konkiewitz is a member of the postgraduate program in Health Sciences at UFGD, researching the cognitive and neuropsychiatric effects of HIV infection. She dedicates herself to writing about medical and scientific topics in her blog, Neurosciences in Debate (Neurociências em Debate) and through videos on diverse subjects related to Neurology and Psychiatry on her channel in YouTube.

Elisabete practices yoga, and has two sons, Marcelo and Lucas Maurício.

Edward Ziff received a bachelor's degree in Chemistry from Columbia University in 1963 and a PhD from Princeton University in Biochemistry in 1969. As a postdoctoral student with Nobel Prize winner, Fred Sanger, in Cambridge he conducted early genome sequencing studies. Ed served on the faculties of the Imperial Cancer Research Fund in London and Rockefeller University in New York. In 1982, he joined New York University School of Medicine, where he is Professor of Biochemistry and Molecular Pharmacology and Neural Science and was an Investigator of the Howard Hughes Medical Institute. Ed researches brain function and neurological disease and was a Visiting Researcher at UFGD in Dourados. He lives in New York, has written for The New York Review of Books, coauthored a popular book on DNA, and is an amateur photographer, video maker, and painter.

Dedication

We dedicate this book to people on the autism spectrum and to their families. We hope it will contribute to a wider understanding of the potentials that people may have within the spectrum and to the realization that human beings have no limitations and cannot be sorted into simple categories.

Acknowledgments

Elisabete would like to thank Camila's parents, Eliana Falchi Parra Carvalho da Silva and José Antônio Carvalho da Silva, who have supported and encouraged her greatly during the writing of this book; the art teacher Gisele Villanova Benages, with whom Camila found her passion for painting, and especially Camila herself, who has provided Elisabete with a new perspective on autism and the human mind with her rich universe of images.

Ed would like to thank his many students and collaborators for their encouragement and support of his investigations in neurobiology, which led to his current interest in autism. In particular, he would like to thank Elisabete for introducing him to Camila Falchi and her art, and the faculty and students at UFGD for their generous hospitality and for many stimulating discussions of the brain.

The authors would like to thank Ms. Pâmela Berton Costa and Ms. Bruna Rafael Neira Muñoz for translation and formatting of the manuscript, and David Ziff for a critical reading of the manuscript and helpful suggestions.

Contents

Foreword 10

1. About Cacá Silva **14**

2. How Many Colors Are in the Spectrum? All of Them and More: Cacá Silva's Artwork **15**

3. Processing Social Information: Grasping What Goes Beyond Logic **18**

What is social information and why do we need it? 18

What are emotion and social cues? 18

Prosody and the expression of emotional cues in speech 19

How do we process emotion and what physiological processes do emotions induce? 22

The hypothalamus, vasopressin and oxytocin 22

4. The Autism Spectrum: Neurons, Brain and Behavior **25**

A brief summary 25

The contribution of genetics 25

Brain development 26

Defining and universal aspects 28

Babies and children on the spectrum: neurodevelopment and behavior 28

Restricted interests, obsessions, and brilliance 31

The difficulty to empathize for a systemizing mind 32

Social understanding and theory of mind 32

How can we test for theory of mind? 35

The false belief test suggests that autistic people lack theory of mind 36

Regions of the brain that are active during theory of mind and their functions 36

How is brain activity affected by autism? 38

5. A New View: Seeing Talents and Opportunities for Integration – Art, Intelligence and Creativity **43**

Music and painting: two welcoming refuges 43

Effectiveness of music and painting: because the autistic mind perceives a different world ... 44

Each person has his or her own spectrum: an individualized look at the choices for therapy and the importance of treating concomitant disorders 47

Adjusting behavior versus building relationships: the importance of early treatment and the controversy over ABA 50

Verbal and alternative communication 53

Cognitive behavioral therapy 55

Sensory processing and sensory integration therapy 56

Animal-assisted therapy 58

Music and art therapy: breaking the shell and finding the pearl 59

Adolescence and adult life: socialization, socioemotional abilities training, and sexuality 62

A misunderstood intelligence profile 67

Can people with ASD be creative? 70

The normal brain is a myth: Asperger syndrome and neurodiversity 74

The school as a space for opportunities: integration, bullying, and peer-mediated interventions 76

Employment as a space of opportunity: all types of thinking can be constructive 80

6. Final Thoughts **84**

7. The Words of a Mother **87**

8. References **92**

Illustrations

I. Eye ("Olho") 9

II. The Web ("A Teia") 12

III. Another Life ("Outra Vida") 13

IV. Origin ("Origem") 17

V. The Rainbow ("O Arco Íris") 20

VI. Gorgeous ("Maravilhosa") 21

VII. The Layers ("As Películas") 24

VIII. The Ball ("A Bola") 27

IX. Polka Dot Cycle ("Ciclo de bolinhas") 30

X. The Dark World ("O Mundo Sombrio") 33

XI. Squares ("Quadrados") 34

XII. Life ("Vida") 37

XIII. Future ("Futuro") 40

XIV. Spring ("Primavera") 42

XV. Ice ("Gelo") 45

XVI. Beauty ("A linda") 48

XVII. Circle of Polka Dots ("Ciclo de Bolinhas") 51

XVIII. Butterfly ("Borboleta") 54

XIX. Labyrinth ("Labirinto") 57

XX. Time ("Tempo") 60

XXI. Sunset ("Pôr do Sol") 63

XXII. Path ("Caminho") 66

XXIII. Happiness ("Felicidade") 69

XXIV. Hallows ("Relíquias") 72

XXV. Earth ("Terra") 75

XXVI. My Family ("Minha Família") 78

XXVII. Hot Air Balloon ("Balão") 81

XXVIII. Hope ("A Esperança") 83

XXIX. World ("Mundo") 86

XXX. Imagination ("Imaginação") 89

XXXI. Brazil ("Brasil") 91

I. Eye ("Olho")

35 cm x 35 cm – acrylic paint, 2014

"***Eye*** – a radiant center of energy, something precious enclosed by circles of fire, a rare gemstone, something quite intense and extraordinary. And the riddle is even more intriguing when you consider that Cacá, along with many people on the spectrum, usually does not make eye contact. The picture, however, may indicate a very particular and sensitive way of perceiving the power in other people's eyes." Elisabete Castelon Konkiewitz (ECK)

"I want the light that comes from within; I want colors to represent emotions." Vincent van Gogh

"I simply thought of an eye." Cacá Silva

Foreword

First, this is a book about art: the art of painting. It is about savoring beauty, feeling sensory joy and taking visual delight. The reader should skim this book freely, without method or rules, and simply enjoy the unpretentious beauty of the pictures. We hope this will be a gentle and relaxing activity, and that your mind can rest and answers can emerge fluidly and intuitively, with no intellectual intervention.

Second, this book tells through images the story of the artist Camila Falchi, who is on the Autism Spectrum Disorder (ASD). Her paintings are evidence of the complexity of her internal world and its variety of themes, intensity of feelings, daydreaming, fantasy and dreams. This complexity is precisely what compels us to question and rethink our perceptions of the autism spectrum, the mind, and creativity. That is why this is, third, a book about the brain, about neuroscience and cognition. Our goal is to disseminate knowledge on autism, its characteristics and potentials, by means of the example of this artist.

Elisabete first met Camila Falchi and became familiar with her paintings in 2014 through her brother, Marcelo Falchi Parra Carvalho Silva, who was one of Elisabete's medical students at UFGD at the time. Their meeting resulted in two art exhibitions during the second and third meetings of the International Grand Dourados Neuroscience Symposium, in 2014 and 2015, respectively. These exhibitions had a very positive outcome, as they brought a new identity for Camila to light. Camila began identifying herself, and being seen by others, as an artist. The exhibitions, at which Edward first met Camila and viewed her art, revealed a talent that was already evident. The outer layer of her former image, based only on her special needs, was partially ruptured and gave way to a sparkle previously unknown.

This book could simply display Camila's paintings, with no portrayal of the autism spectrum, as their strength and beauty are enough to enchant the public and to convince people of their aesthetic value. However, the autism spectrum is discussed herein precisely because these paintings, so vibrant and intense, break stereotypes, reveal an unappreciated emotional universe, and bring forth new directions to thoughts and actions concerning autism.

The book starts with a brief introduction to Camila Falchi, in Chapter 1, and remarks on her art, in Chapter 2. Chapter 3 considers how the brain processes social information, a capacity that may present a challenge for persons on the spectrum. Chapter 4 comments on the autism spectrum with up-to-date information on its prevalence, manifestation, diagnosis, and new cognitive models that explain it both in its deficit aspects and in its specific talents. We discuss perceptual, emotional and attentional aspects of autism in terms of the role of genetics and autism susceptibility genes and their contributions to the origins of ASD.

We explore how psychological and imaging studies of the social brain using the most modern techniques have revealed differences between neurotypicals (those not on the autism spectrum) and ASD persons and how these studies have provided new insights into the fundamentals of social interaction, such as how we develop concepts of the relationship between ourselves and others. We review what has been learned from clinical studies of how the autistic brain is distinguished in its development, neurophysiology and psychology. Chapter 5 discusses how a person on the autism spectrum has particular visual and auditory perceptions, his or her own interest profile, intense focus, and lasting attention abilities, which should not be considered only as weaknesses, but in some instances may be strengths. Even verbal communication and emotional understanding difficulties may have a positive side if, when they cause isolation, they provide freedoms that arise from independence from social groups. We highlight painting and music as means of personal expression that are particularly attractive for people on the spectrum and adapted to the autistic mind and thus offer unusual opportunities. Art therapy and music therapy are then discussed as promising possibilities for complementing therapies based on behavior adaptation and modification, such as psycho-therapy, language-therapy, animal-assisted therapy and sensory integration therapy. We also discuss social challenges in adolescence. We go on to propose that the concepts and means for evaluation of intelligence and creativity within the spectrum be revised to reveal how these potentials of the autism group have been consistently underestimated In this context, Neurodiversity is an awareness movement that demands more participation by people on the autism spectrum in society as well as their inclusion in schools and in the job market, and, above all, the application of new concepts of normalcy and mental health. In Chapter 6, we place Camila and her paintings into a greater perspective based on what we have learned about the causes of autism and based on our hopes for how persons on the spectrum may be integrated into our educational system and into society. Finally, the book ends in Chapter 7 with the testimony of Camila's mother about her path of fight and achievement. It is without doubt a story of love and courage

II. The Web ("A Teia")

60 cm x 120 cm – acrylic paint, 2015

"Color is a power which directly influences the soul." Wassily Kandinsky

"I wanted to paint a spider, but it didn't really work, so I painted the spider's web." Cacá Silva

III. Another Life ("Outra Vida") 40 cm x 50 cm – colored glue over acrylic paint, 2013

"Another Life – This painting's theme is of a spiritual nature and displays consciousness of the transience of life and loss, and also the conviction that such things are a cycle. The background of this cosmic game consists of warm colors, like the embrace of a Great Mother." ECK

"A work of art is the expression of a reality, something on its wholesome and with no correspondence to the conscious intentions of the author." Georges Braque

"It means being born again." Cacá Silva

1. About Cacá Silva

Camila Falchi Parra Carvalho Silva was born on March 28, 1991, in Votuporanga, SP, Brazil, and lives with her parents and her sister Beatriz, in São José do Rio Preto, SP, Brazil. Besides painting, which she has practiced since 2009 with her teacher Gisele Villanova Benages, Camila plays the piano and is especially interested in movies and animals, subjects present in both her daily life and her artwork. Her favorite movies are *Harry Potter* and *Lord of the Rings*, which she has watched many times, as she owns both complete collections, along with the *Twilight* series.

However, the world is not always so simple for Camila. At times, small everyday decisions can present a distressful dilemma. Obsessive–compulsive disorder (OCD) makes objects or isolated words seem to have peculiar and ominous meanings, forcing Camila to go through long and tormenting rituals. At times, she cannot even tell what is causing her anxiety, leaving her only with the need to obey her compulsions. Despite this, Camila is a happy and self-reliant young woman. She is even-tempered, placid, affective, and cheerful. She knows her own story and does not consider herself as "someone with a problem", but rather as a person with some limitations, as normal as anyone else. She has great self-esteem. Even if not particularly vain, she considers herself beautiful and enjoys socialization.

2. How Many Colors Are in the Spectrum? All of Them and More: Cacá Silva's Artwork

Camila Falchi's pictorial universe is, above all, a colorful universe. Colors are the protagonists and a means of expression. There is no perspective, no volume, no light or shadow nuances. Composition results from the combination of colors in simple and clear shapes, with no monochromatic overlay, but instead mostly contrasting with each other. They are bright, intense colors and, most of the time, the colors are distinct. The lines are not geometrical, but irregular, curvilinear, and casually asymmetrical, which makes them cozier, more human, and less stiff.

Even when supposedly representing an external object, the composition only refers to the object as an initial inspiration and does not actually portray such an object. The paintings seem to follow their own directions, always towards the interior universe. There is no conceptual formulation or planning and no restraints. What happens is a fluid activity, one that is highly concentrated and intuitive.

Camila does not seem to have inhibitions or to fear mistakes. Her art is created spontaneously, with no regrets or corrections. The vivid colors, vibrant contrasts, and thick lines expose this pulsating and impulsive energy. For example, the beautiful *The Web* (page 12) is improvised, as Camila herself explains: "I wanted to paint a spider, but it didn't really work, so I painted the spider's web." This is proof of great cognitive flexibility and emotional balance when Camila is met with frustration, characteristics that are not expected since persons on the spectrum are more commonly rigid in their behavior.

Camila's vision of her own work and artistic process is just as spontaneous. She does not submit her artworks to intellectual analysis and she does not try to explain, justify, or even understand them. When asked about the thought processes behind certain paintings, her answers are often "I don't know", or they can be so direct and simple that the interlocutor starts doubting the question itself. For instance, regarding the painting, *The Eye* (page 09), she answers: "I simply thought of an eye." It is as if she said "can't you see it is an eye? Well, what else would it be?" She leaves the interpretation of complexity and multiple meanings of the pictures she creates for those who want to spend their time on such things, and that indifference and even unawareness grant her freedom and authenticity. None of it is created to have a deeper meaning or to defend an ideal.

Camila Falchi is fascinated by certain shapes, which appear repeatedly in her paintings, such as polka dots, squares, circles, and parallel and divergent lines. These shapes and the colors themselves are already the theme, and are not necessarily referencing something else. To name her paintings or to explain her work is the artist's way of conceding to our need for interpretation. In fact, Camila is entertained for hours by her polka dots and lines, spots and circles. For her, they are already imbued with their own singular meanings. Their endless possibilities of variation and combination make up a universe that is self-sufficient. These preferences are not a limitation; in fact, her work is quite varied and it confirms both a will to experiment and the receptiveness to the unknown of an optimist with a curious spirit.

The abstract aspect of her paintings establishes an environment of expression and communication on an intuitive, immediate, and illogical level. It is like a window to a free flow of mental associations and emotional states. The viewer is compelled to observe the painting and may try to decipher it and translate it into words, but what catches the eye is the beauty, purely resulting from colors and shapes. There is no explanation, only experience. Therefore, the comments on Camila's work should not be considered an exegesis, but simply a subjective and very personal response to them. Any attempt to interpret the paintings psychologically would likely be naive and erroneous.

IV. Origin ("Origem") 40 cm x 60 cm – colored glue and acrylic paint, 2013

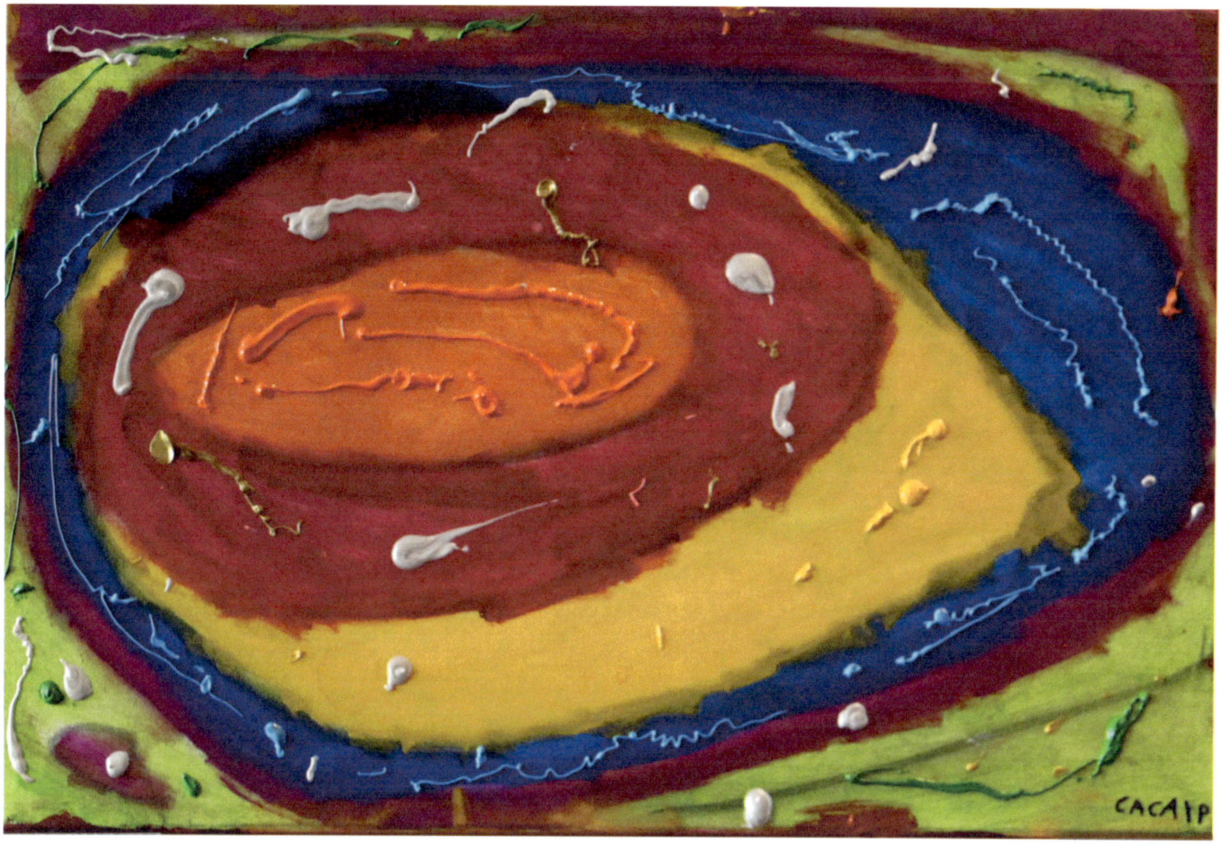

"***Origin*** – A large egg with many protective layers and life being formed in its center, or many spermatozoa carrying the hope of fecundation and of new life, or the unending expansion and contraction cycle of the universe." ECK

"Painting is self-discovery. Every good artist paints what he is." Jackson Pollock

"It means a lot, the origin of things, for example, the origin of life." Cacá Silva

3. Processing Social Information: Grasping What Goes Beyond Logic

What is social information and why do we need it?

People on the spectrum often exhibit behaviors and social interactions that puzzle neurotypical persons (those not on the autism spectrum) and that may impair their participation in social situations. To begin to understand the origins of autism and the challenges it poses for persons with autism spectrum disorders (ASDs) and neurotypical alike, we must consider how autism affects social communication and behavior. Although autism takes many forms, people on the spectrum often do not recognize or respond to social signals from others and lack ability to communicate their own social signals. Therefore, to start to understand the social challenges of autism, we must consider how these forms of social communication take place and the purposes they serve.

Because we are social beings and we live in a highly socially interconnected world, we must be sensitive to the feelings and social needs of family, friends, coworkers and other members of our community to navigate our daily lives successfully. Feelings and social needs are often expressed indirectly through verbal and nonverbal social cues. If we can recognize these social cues and take them into account, our lives will become more harmonious. To achieve social harmony, we must also be able to project our own social cues so that others may appreciate our own needs and emotions.

What are emotion and social cues?

Social cues reflect emotions, which are mental states that organize and simplify our reactions to social situations and that have numerous physiological correlates. Ideally, we perceive the emotions of others accurately. To do so, when presented with an emotional stimulus, we must be able to appraise it and determine its nature and strength (Phillips, Drevets, Rauch, & Lane, 2003). In fact, the brain receives copious amounts of information of all sorts, not just information about emotion. Our brains receive information about people we work and socialize with, about places we frequent, the food we eat, and the things that give us pleasure or pain. We receive this information through visual, auditory, olfactory, taste and tactile sensations etc. provided by our senses. The brain must organize and comprehend this information. Notably, we can recognize objects (a car, a spoon, an apple), even if we have never seen that particular car, spoon or apple before by realizing that the object belongs to a category or a group with which we are already familiar. Likewise, the human mind has a profound capacity to understand the mental states of others through recognition of verbal and nonverbal cues indicating anger, enthusiasm, affection or disdain, even if we have only just met the person. Just as we recognize a car, a spoon or an apple from its general features, we recognize emotions when projected by particular visual cues, such as a raised eyebrow or pursed lips or other facial expressions, or by stance and gestures. Facial expressions are particularly informative and one way we understand them is to mimic them (A. Wood, Rychlowska, Korb, & Niedenthal, 2016). When someone smiles, we smile!

Prosody and the expression of emotional cues in speech

We also recognize verbal cues, which are incorporated into our speech through our tone of voice or choice of language. Some verbal cues are conveyed in the form of prosody. Prosody refers to aspects of speech that are beyond vowels and consonants. Prosody refers to the pitch, intensity, and speed of speaking (Ross, 2010). When the emotional side of prosody, the expression of verbal emotional cues, is impaired, interpersonal relations suffer because speech without prosody sounds mechanical and is annoying. Likewise, a listener who is emotionally insensitive may fail to recognize social cues provided by prosody, leading to inappropriate behavior that also impairs social relationships. Interestingly, people with autism who have difficulty interpreting social cues in speech may prefer to communicate with computers and dispense with the social side of communication entirely.

V. The Rainbow ("O Arco Íris")

50 cm x 60 cm – acrylic paint, 2014.

"The ***rainbow*** is distorted and asymmetrical, and this distortion is responsible for the movement and dynamism in the painting. Besides that, the colors do not correspond to those found on a real rainbow. There is briskness, energy, and courage for self-expression, and even some boldness in painting outside the lines." ECK

"I thought about the happiness connected to colors. The rainbow is something happy." Cacá Silva

VI. Gorgeous ("Maravilhosa") 70 cm x 90 cm – colored glue and acrylic paint, 2015

"Composition is an absolute mystery. It is dictated by the mind. The artist searchers for certain sounds or lines that are acceptable to the mind and finally an arrangement of them that is acceptable. The acceptable compositions arouse certain feelings of appreciation in the observer. Some compositions appeal to some, and some to others." Agnes Martin

How do we process emotion and what physiological processes do emotions induce?

Social and emotional cues are powerful because they have profound effects on our bodies and our minds. We respond to these cues by releasing hormones, by changing the activity of our nervous system and by adjusting body expression, such as by smiling, frowning, gasping, or laughing. To understand how we communicate socially, we need to understand how we form these mental and visceral responses.

Functional magnetic resonance imaging (fMRI), a powerful technique that maps active regions of the brain, has revealed a central role for a brain region named the prefrontal cortex in processing social cues. The prefrontal cortex provides "executive functions", such as weighing the merits of alternative actions, generating goal-directed behavior and predicting the outcomes of these behaviors, all of which are processes that take place when we assess the emotions of others. Significantly, function of the prefrontal cortex is often impaired in autistic persons, a point that we discuss extensively below. Another brain region that processes social cues, the hypothalamus, communicates information from the brain to the body to control bodily physiological processes. Brain regions that provide pain perception also process social cues

The hypothalamus, vasopressin and oxytocin

The hypothalamus has a major role in deciphering social and emotional signals and inducing appropriate behaviors (Insel, 2010). The hypothalamus is well known for readying the body for immanent attack, to which we may respond by fight or by flight respectively by committing acts of aggression or avoidance. The hypothalamus also responds to positive interpersonal interactions by preparing us to "tend and befriend" and to engage in sexual interaction and play. The hypothalamus releases two peptides, oxytocin and arginine vasopressin (AVP), that control social behavior. In rats, oxytocin induces maternal behavior, such as grooming of pups, and oxytocin exerts these maternal behavior effects even when it is injected into a virgin female rat, which would otherwise be hostile to the pups. Another form of social control is induced by AVP in voles, which are small, mouse-like mammals. Some strains of voles are monogamous, and with monogamous voles, AVP produced by the hypothalamus induces pair bonding after mating, a kind of monogamy that includes partner preference, guarding of the mate from attack and sharing the care of the pups between the mother and the father.

It is clear that chemical signals released by the hypothalamus exert strong control over social behaviors. Of these signals, oxytocin has raised great interest for autism because of the numerous forms of social behavior it mediates (Maroun & Wagner, 2016). Oxytocin is released from a subregion of the hypothalamus and is required for a special form of memory called social recognition memory. In rodents, social memory enables a mouse or rat to recall individual animals, often through their odor, and then to focus their attention on other, new and novel mice or rats. Elimination of the oxytocin gene from a mouse prevents the formation of long-term social recognition memory.

Oxytocin regulates many parts of the brain, but the amygdala, a brain region that is associated with emotional memory, is especially important. Oxytocin can induce memories that lead to both socially positive approach behavior and to avoidance behavior, depending on which amygdala region is stimulated. The memories are formed when sensory information arising from smell, sight etc. join in the amygdala with information from the prefrontal cortex, a decision-making brain region. Oxytocin helps these converging incoming activities to modify specific amygdala circuits to form social memories. The balance between positive acting and negative acting regions decides between approach and avoidance behavior.

Because oxytocin can promote pro social behavior, it is a candidate drug for improving sociability of autistic children. In promising initial trials, administration of oxytocin to autistic children through a nasal spray improved social behaviors (Evans, Dal Monte, Noble, & Averbeck, 2014). Undoubtedly, other new medications for treating autism will emerge as our understanding of the physiological basis for autism increases.

VII. The Layers ("As Películas") 40 cm x 50 cm – black glue, acrylic paint, 2010

"Things do not exist on their own. They only exist through us." Georges Braque

4. The Autism Spectrum: Neurons, Brain and Behavior

A brief summary

Most people are born with the brain functions that allow them to learn spontaneously and easily, to learn how to communicate with other people, and to learn how to understand the rules of society and behavioral conventions. This learning process is essential to being accepted in society and to adapting to it. Skills such as knowing how to request help, how to invite others for a group game, how to comfort others, and how to share experiences are what bring us together and allow for the formation of cultural identities.

These are precisely the main defining characteristics of the ASD, which has been recognized as a neurobiological developmental disorder that is linked to communication and socialization impairments and to repetitive behavior with restricted interests (American Psychiatric Association, 2013).

ASD has become a topic of general interest and concern because of its high and rapidly rising prevalence. In the United States, it is estimated that one out of every 68 children is autistic (National Center on Birth Defects and Developmental Disabilities, 2014), a rate 30% higher than in 2008 (1 in every 88), 60% higher than in 2006 (1 in every 110), and 120% higher than in 2000 and 2002 (1 in every 150). There is still no scientific explanation for this alarming phenomenon, and simple changes in evaluation and diagnostic criteria are not enough to explain such a sudden rise in the number of cases. Despite the lack of data in Brazil, the prevalence of autism is acknowledged to be high and possibly close to the prevalence in the United States. ASD affects all ethnicities and is approximately five times more common among men.

The contribution of genetics

The cause of ASD is currently unknown; however, it is clearly a disorder of neurobiological nature with a strong genetic contribution. Monozygotic twins exhibit a rate of concordance between .62 and .94, which means that if one of them has autism, the other has a risk between 62% and 94% of having it as well. For the siblings of people with autism, there is a 10% risk, which is a lot lower than for people sharing the same genetic material (monozygotic twins), but still a lot higher than for the general population (around 1.4%). However, the genetics of autism are complex, for it is not caused by a single gene, but by a great number of different variables that together create the spectrum (Barnard, Pomaville, & O'Roak, 2015).

Exacting studies of DNA from families with a high incidence of autism have identified about two hundred genes whose mutations increase the incidence of autism (de la Torre Ubieta, Won, Stein, & Geschwind,

2016). At first glance, no clear common factor connects the functions of these genes apart from the fact that many are expressed in the brain. Indeed, some of the autism susceptibility genes encode proteins that help neurons adhere to each other, while others encode scaffolds that stabilize synapses, while yet others encode proteins that communicate signals within or between neurons and several others control complex programs of neuronal gene activity. Some coherence emerges in this gene set if we take into account that autism is a developmental disorder, and that the autism susceptibility genes are all required in one way or another for the development of a fully functional brain. When autism susceptibility genes are mutated, the mutations may disrupt aspects of brain development, leading to autism.

Brain development

Development of a functional brain is a process of staggering complexity. First, the brain must organize numerous different types of neurons into specific functional clusters, layers and sheets. In this process, newly generated neurons migrate from the sites of their "birth" within the developing brain to particular destinations, where they begin to function. Once in place, they must be connected to one another through the formation of synapses to generate functional circuits. To form the mature, adult brain, synapses must be created in vast numbers, totaling perhaps as many as a million billion of them (10^{15}). Synapses are points of contact between neurons at which one neuron communicates with another. Notably, there are more synapses in one human brain than there are stars in our galaxy! The integrity of synapse formation relies on the fidelity of the proteins that orchestrate the formation of synapses. Mutation of genes that encode synapse-forming proteins lead to expression of altered forms of these proteins that are usually defective. Mutation of autism susceptibility genes can potentially have many effects on brain development. Some mutations may alter the number of neurons that are produced during development, influence the migration of neurons into functional groups, or disrupt the formation of synapses. Mutant genes encoding proteins with even slight errors in structure, when expressed repeatedly in developing brain's myriad of neurons and associated synapses, can throw the brain's circuits out of balance, cloud the brain's signaling pathways and cause the system to operate abnormally. Studies show that genetically based autism is polygenic, that is, genetically based forms of autism are caused not by mutation of a single gene but by a confluence of gene mutations that modify each other's impact. Given the potentially enormous number of combinations of mutant genes that could arise, with each combination having its own special consequences, it is not surprising that autism is a spectrum of disorders.

Other causes, apart from genetic ones, have been proposed for the origins of autism and indeed, it is likely that nongenetic causes play a significant role. However, it is important to emphasize that the belief by some that ASD could in any way result from maternal behavior is no longer accepted. Psychologist Bruno Bettelheim proposed during the 1950's and 1960's, the theory that maternal indifference (refrigerator mother) could be

VIII. The Ball ("A Bola") 40 cm x 40 cm – glue over acrylic paint, 2012

"This world of imagination is fancy-free and violently opposed to common sense." Mark Rothko

"I was simply inspired by a ball." Cacá Silva

the cause for a child's change in behavior, but he disproved and disavowed this theory decades later. Sadly, this explanation is still widely spread in popular belief, causing misunderstanding and shame, and reducing access of ASD individuals to effective therapies.

Defining and universal aspects

In fact, ASD refers to a quite heterogeneous group when it comes to ability profiles, personal obstacles, and behavioral patterns, ranging from people with severe intellectual disability who are not capable of communicating verbally or developing any degree of independence, to highly intelligent people who are professionally successful and socially adapted. However, despite this heterogeneity, defining and universal aspects of ASD exist, and are: 1) difficulty in communicating and having social interactions, including expression of minimal social responses; 2) struggle to identify other people's emotions and intentions; and 3) a pattern of restricted and repetitive behaviors.

There is no specific brain alteration always linked to ASD that is visible, for example, through neuroimaging or electrophysiological examinations. Therefore, the diagnosis of autism is purely clinical, based on reports of caregivers and on analysis of the child's behavior. Ultimately, several complementary examinations may be required to evaluate the presence of possible concomitant disorders (Schwartzman, 2015).

Babies and children on the spectrum: neurodevelopment and behavior

It has become increasingly feasible to detect signs of ASD at very early ages, and this may be possible even during the first year of life. For instance, babies with autism tend to make less eye contact with their mothers and other people. They tend to dislike being touched, to respond less often when called, and to rely less on their mothers for comfort or safety. They also exhibit a deficit in shared attention activities, in which two or more people focus on the same object that is external to themselves. For example, if we see someone looking up, our natural response is to look in the same direction. Likewise, during games based on persons taking turns (chess, table tennis, circle games, musical games with rhymes and movement), the players most often remain focused on a common element. However, babies with autism do not share interest in an object of attention indicated by other people; for example, they do not look in the direction his or her mother points, and do not participate in games initiated by her.

During their development, children with ASD frequently exhibit language acquisition delay. Besides struggling to form phrases, they can exhibit other difficulties, such as echolalia (repetition of what they have just heard) or difficulty in referring to themselves as I, using their own name or third-person pronouns instead. As we have noted in Chapter 3 (Prosody and the expression of emotional cues in speech), their prosody (intonation with which phrases are pronounced) can be monotonous or artificial, and their speech can be sung or enunciated in a way that is odd and stereotyped, and that may lack the expected vocal variations that transmit emotions. Even after acquiring moderate vocabulary and grammatical concepts, their language can be too formal, rigid and unexpressive, and they may have great difficulty in understanding figures of speech, such as slang and metaphor.

Children with ASD may make repetitive, purposeless movements, such as rocking their arms, head, or body. They are frequently fixated upon certain rituals that cannot be altered. For example they may resist changes in furniture placement in a room, the bus route to school, where they sit in class, pieces of clothing they wear, a specific food they eat, and there may be words that must be said at certain moments and words that must not be said, etc. Any small change could cause agitation, extreme anxiety, or even self-harm. As the child cannot properly articulate what is troubling him or her, and as the other do not usually notice the change that causes the difficulty, his or her behavior remains uncomprehended and the child cannot be comforted.

Children with ASD may have a deficit in imagination that can be observed in the way they play. Such children explore objects by setting them in a line, spinning them, bumping them together, etc., but these playthings usually are not imagined as objects of a different sort. The banana does not turn into a phone, shoes do not turn into cars, and tree leaves do not turn into food for their toys. They are rarely interested in fictional stories such as fairy tales, movies, theater plays, and cartoons. At times, a story character can fascinate them, so they copy the character's clothing, habits, and speech patterns, for example, but they do not seem to be involved with the character's emotional universe. What is lacking is the "theory of mind", which is the understanding of other people's feelings, beliefs, intentions, and motivations, and the comprehension that they are separate from one's own interior state. For example, when watching a movie in which someone suffers because of believing in a lie, we are capable of identifying and understanding the cause of suffering while simultaneously knowing that the character is the victim of an illusion and that the movie itself has no correspondence with reality. Despite knowing about the lie in the plot and that the story itself is not real, we are capable of–and even enjoy–putting ourselves in the character's emotional state and even suffering along with them. However, a person with ASD would have trouble separating the plot's reality, which is shared with the viewer, from the lie that the character believes in.

Children with ASD also do not play pretend, because pretending requires playing certain roles and using theory of mind to infer the proper reactions and behaviors required for each role. Shared attention is also necessary for play pretend, as the children will share the same "lie" in an implicit pact. By being aware that all of them are "lying", they can be the actors, directors, and screenwriters at the same time, a practice that provides training for different social situations.

IX. Polka Dot Cycle ("Ciclo de bolinhas")

50 cm x 70 cm – acrylic paint, 2014

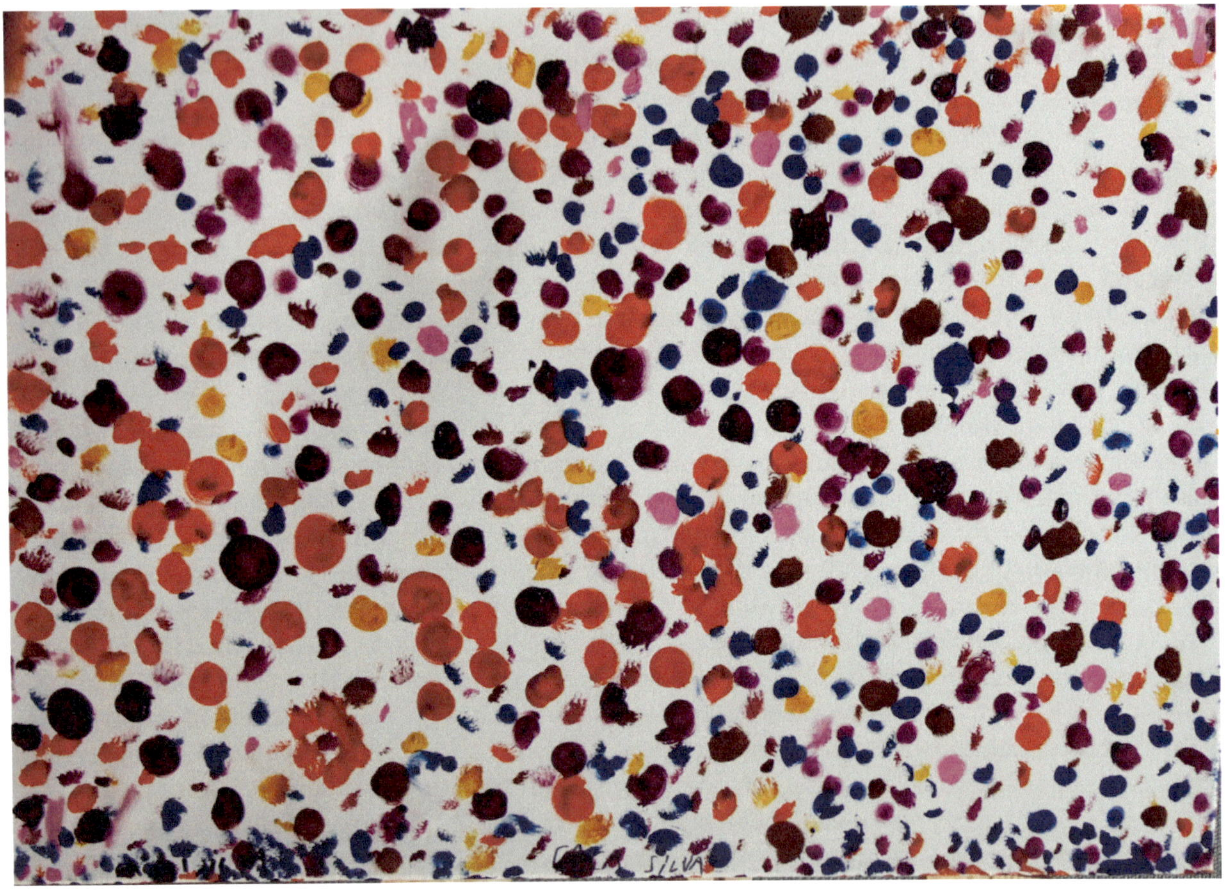

"... I'm not sure, I think about polka dots, about the things I like, and I like polka dots, so I find the colors I like, sort them out and paint, I don't know." Yayoi Kusama

In short, the series of difficulties in perceiving their surroundings and expressing themselves is what makes socialization much harder and causes children with ASD to be isolated–despite most being truly well-meaning, honest, sincere, and often intelligent, affable, and even funny individuals–and causes them to have little chance of fully developing and offering their contributions to the world.

Restricted interests, obsessions, and brilliance

ASD, despite all scientific efforts, is still fundamentally an enigma to the neurosciences and psychology, a fascinating mystery that however is defined not only by an individual's limitations, but also by talents and particular capabilities. For example, restricted interests, traditionally considered incapacitating, may be advantageous under certain circumstances. People with ASD are capable of being entertained for hours by an activity that, to an outsider, would appear to be repetitive, boring, and senseless, such as spinning an object, watching water fall or lights glimmer, or by observing geometric and colored patterns, or by numerical combinations, etc. At times, this intense and even obsessive fascination can result in extraordinary accomplishments. It is estimated that around 30% of people with autism exhibit some degree of savantism, which is to say, prodigious capacities, most commonly in music, drawing, performing calendar calculations, memory, spatial navigation and computer skills (Treffert & Rebedew, 2015).

The term savant syndrome originally referred to the paradox of someone simultaneously exhibiting evident intellectual deficits and at the same time exhibiting talents in restricted areas that are far superior to even those of an intellectually gifted person. Treffert (2009) suggests the rare cases of "prodigious" savant people (those with absolutely incredible abilities) be differentiated from the more frequent cases of "talented" savant people (those whose performance in an isolated area is surprising when compared to the global cognitive profile). Nowadays, savantism itself is understood to occupy a wide spectrum, which means that specific talents can be found at many different levels.

There are numerous cases of pianists, painters, and brilliant mathematicians who have been diagnosed with ASD. Practice of a skill, which requires the ability to keep intense and lasting focus, enables one to perceive details most often overlooked, to change perspective, to deconstruct, to reconstruct, to test, and, finally, to produce works of value. It is possible that people on the autism spectrum get more easily into the "state of flow", a condition described by Csíkszentmihályi and Lefevre (1989) as being fully immersed in an activity, with a reduced perception of time, environment, and even physical needs such as food, sleep, or rest. This state is seen as highly pleasurable, one that produces an ideal experience that is intrinsically motivating.

The difficulty to empathize for a systemizing mind

The exact same variations in the autistic brain that lead to difficulty in communication and socialization can be associated with perception and cognitive processes that provide certain advantages and abilities. According to the Empathizing–Systemizing Theory proposed by Simon Baron-Cohen, E. Ashwin, C. Ashwin, Tavassoli, and Chakrabarti (2009), the autistic brain has a great tendency for systemizing, which is to say, a great tendency to search for rules within the environmental stimuli, making it possible to group, sort, and predict these stimuli. Some examples are to group numbers according to certain rules (e.g., prime numbers, numbers divisible by seven); to group animals according to a shared characteristic; to sort words into alphabetical order, etc. Simultaneously, people on the spectrum often exhibit a deficit in empathy, a deficit in the ability to formulate responses and behaviors appropriate to the thoughts and emotions of others, abilities that require multiple levels of socioemotional processing. To function effectively socially, it is essential to comprehend the points of view of others and to know that the mental states of other people are separate and different from one's own (theory of mind). One must understand different social contexts and, finally, one must formulate behaviors adequate for interaction with others. At times, people with ASD are capable of recognizing someone else's emotional state, but they do not know how to react to that state, resulting in excessive honesty, tactlessness, dullness, and awkwardness during social interactions.

Social understanding and theory of mind

Our understanding of the neural origins of autism dates back to the historic paper by Leo Kanner, *Autistic Disturbances of Affective Contact*, published in 1943, which first described autism as a distinct syndrome. Today, our knowledge of autism has increased exponentially, and autism is understood to involve changes in specific brain circuits and mutations of particular genes. As research on autism has crystallized around specific molecular, genetic and physiological alterations of the brain that can be investigated with powerful, new research tools, more and more investigators have been drawn to the field. Some of the most provoking recent studies involve theory of mind, a brain process that, as we have noted in Chapter 4 (Babies and children on the spectrum: neurodevelopment and behavior), enables us to engage in play pretend, to immerse ourselves in the plot of a novel or in fanciful group activities. This theory, which makes it possible for us to understand emotional and mental states of others, is altered in ASD. Studies of theory of mind have provided important clues to the complex origins of autism.

Theory of mind, most simply stated, is the hypothesis we make in our own minds about what is going on in the mind of another, a kind of educated guess about other people's thoughts and emotions. Theory of mind is a part of our own consciousness, a personal state known only to the particular individual, thus difficult–perhaps impossible–for another to know or even to measure. Nonetheless, psychologists and

X. The Dark World ("O Mundo Sombrio") 30 cm x 50 cm – acrylic paint, 2015

"If there were only one truth, you couldn't paint a hundred canvases on the same theme." Pablo Picasso
"This is how I see the world, each person sees it however they want." Cacá Silva

XI. Squares ("Quadrados")

40 cm x 60 cm – acrylic paint, 2015

"The painting rises from the brush strokes as the poem rises from the words. The meaning comes later." Joan Miró neurobiologists have worked hard to establish objective tests for theory of mind, in order to place its study on a scientific basis. Using such tests, researchers have asked, at what age do we acquire the ability to form theory of mind? Which parts of the brain provide this function and do different people form theory of mind differently? The answers led to the conclusion that ASD individuals do not form theory of mind as do neuro-typical persons and that in autistic persons, the functions of specific brain regions related to theory of mind appear to be altered.

How can we test for theory of mind?

A seminal paper published in 1978 by Premack and Woodruff asked whether chimpanzees understand human goals and if they express psychological states that humans express, such as "*purpose* or *intention*, as well as *knowledge, belief, thinking, doubt, guessing, pretending, liking*" (Premack and Woodruff, 1978). In their study, Premack and Woodruff showed chimpanzees videotapes of humans attempting to solve a problem, such as struggling to grasp a banana or other food. Then they gave the chimpanzees the chance to choose between two photographs, one showing a solution to the human's problem, such as a stick for reaching for the bananas, and the other an irrelevant photograph. Because the chimpanzees consistently chose the photograph showing the solution, the investigators concluded that the chimpanzees could understand what was going on in the mind of the human in the videotape. Premack and Woodruff referred to this understanding by the chimpanzees of the thoughts of the humans as theory of mind. They chose this name because neither the chimpanzee (nor indeed a human) could be certain of what is going on in the mind of another, and thus the chimpanzee could at best have a "theory" about the mental state of the human grasping for food.

The Premack and Woodruff paper was highly controversial, but it stimulated extensive discussion about the nature of theory of mind (Schaafsma, Pfaff, Spunt, & Adolphs, 2015) and what form it took in people. Because theory of mind is an aspect of consciousness, and it is widely accepted that we cannot directly experience the consciousness of others, detecting and measuring theory of mind in humans required new and sophisticated tests.

In the early tests for theory of mind, a subject was asked if another person held a particular belief, a belief that could be true or false. The philosopher, Daniel Dennett, however suggested that a prediction by the subject that the other person held a "true" belief would not be a sufficient test. The subject might reach that conclusion just by analyzing the facts of the case, rather than by analyzing the thought processes of the other person. Dennett (1978) proposed instead that the subject should predict that another person maintained a belief that was in fact false. The author held that a subject would have to perceive the state of mind of the other person to reach this conclusion.

Following Dennett's suggestion, Wimmer and Perner (1983) devised a now classical test for theory of mind based on false beliefs that could be applied to children. In this test, a child who is being tested observes the following scenario. A person in the scenario, Maxi, places a chocolate into a blue cabinet, and then leaves the room. While Maxi is out of the room, Maxi's mother moves the chocolate to a second, green cabinet. When Maxi returns, the child subject is asked where Maxi will look for the object. A neurotypical child as young as 4 years old will predict that Maxi has the false belief that the object is still in the blue cabinet, and that Maxi will look there, in its original location. Answering this test correctly is accepted as strong evidence that a child has theory of mind (Wimmer & Perner, 1983).

Since this pioneering study, other tests (Perner & Wimmer, 1988) have shown that even an 18 month-old neurotypical child is aware of the mental states of others (reviewed by U. Frith & Frith, 2003) and even younger children have related mental abilities. Because 18 months is the start of a period of rapid brain development, acquisition of theory of mind was deemed strongly dependent on the brain's development processes.

The false belief test suggests that autistic people lack theory of mind

Because people on the spectrum respond differently to the social aspects of others (Jones, Gliga, Bedford, Charman, & Johnson, 2014), researchers asked if theory of mind also differed in ASD persons. To test this possibility, Simon Baron-Cohen of Oxford (who later proposed the Empathizing–Systemizing Theory discussed above), along with Leslie and Frith (1985), applied the "chocolate in the cabinet" false belief test to autistic children and concluded that autistic children don't form a theory of mind, at least not like neurotypical children. The ASD children failed the test at a high rate while neurotypical children correctly recognized that Maxi would have a false belief about the location of the chocolate. Significantly, a majority of Down syndrome children answered the test correctly. Thus Down syndrome children could form a theory of mind, although they had lower intelligence as measured by standard tests. This suggests that forming theory of mind requires something quite different from general intelligence. The finding by Baron-Cohen et al. was intriguing because it suggested that if we could understand theory of mind, we might also understand the unresponsiveness of ASD children to social cues and perhaps autism itself.

Regions of the brain that are active during theory of mind and their functions

To start to understand how the brain forms theory of mind, scientists employed a new technique that emerged in the 1980s called functional magnetic resonance imaging (fMRI). The method measures the flow of oxygen-carrying blood in order to make a three dimensional map of the brain's active regions (Logothetis, Pauls, Augath, Trinath, & Oeltermann, 2001). By imaging the brain while a person performs a task, the relevant brain regions can be identified. These studies were the first to reveal that brain regions for theory of mind function differently in people on the spectrum.

XII. Life ("Vida") 60 cm x 60 cm – colored glue and acrylic paint, 2013

"Life is red and bleeds. Life is voluminous and demands its place. Life occupies its space, life is huge, life is strong. Life does not hide. Life does not cower. Life does not feel embarrassment. Life fights." ECK

"It is quite commonly thought that the intellect is responsible for everything that is made and done. It is commonly thought that everything that is can be put into words. But there is a wide range of emotional response that we make that cannot be put into words. We are so used to making these emotional responses that we are not consciously aware of them until they are represented in artwork." Agnes Martin

When neurobiologists asked neurotypical subjects to read a story that required an understanding of what was going on in the mind of a story character, fMRI indicated increased activity in at least three brain regions (Dichter, 2012). These were the medial prefrontal cortex (MPFC), the posterior superior temporal sulcus (STS) and the temporal poles (TP). Interestingly, all three were parts of the "social brain". As we have already discussed, the MPFC, which is located just behind the forehead, provides executive functions, such as making decisions about how to behave. The MPFC gathers sensory information about a person's immediate situation, such as about the room in which the person is located and the person's position in that room. It receives motor information about the person's actions, such as whether the person is turning or walking. The MPFC also receives information about the events that the individual is experiencing and about the outcomes of past actions taken by the person in similar situations, in particular whether the outcomes were rewarding. Based on all of this information, the MPFC guides us in choosing the action or behavior to perform that would be most beneficial for us at that moment. The STS processes socially relevant sensory information, such as the sound of a voice versus the sound of a machine and the sight of faces or the telling of stories. It also processes how people are directing their attention, as judged by the line of their sight. The TPs process social and emotional information as well. Surgical lesion of the TPs in monkeys causes social withdrawal, failure to recognize vocal or facial social signals from others and failure to produce these signals. As researchers carried out further imaging studies of theory of mind, yet other brain regions were implicated. Strikingly, the theory of mind brain regions were dedicated to social functions of the brain.

The power of fMRI unleashed yet other unexpected findings. Researchers discovered that the brain parts used to generate theory of mind overlap a group of regions that are active when our mind is at rest, collectively called the Default Mode Network (DMN). The DMN becomes active when we are not working on a particular external task, our thoughts about the outside world recede and we engage in introspection, mind-wandering, and daydreaming (Buckner, Andrews-Hanna, & Schacter, 2008). The anatomical overlap of theory of mind and Default Mode Network regions suggested that the way we think about the minds of others is related to the way we assess our own situations and meditate about ourselves.

How is brain activity affected by autism?

The significance of these findings for autism soon became evident. Reading a story that stimulated theory of mind regions in a neurotypical person had a much smaller effect on an ASD person's brain activity (Dichter, 2012). This suggested that when an ASD person is confronted by a need to understand the mind of another, their theory of mind brain regions aren't activated as much as they would be in a neurotypical brain. Furthermore, researchers found that the DMN or mind-wandering network was also controlled differently in ASD persons (Kennedy, Redcay, & Courchesne, 2006). Although the DMN was activated in neurotypicals when their minds were not directed to an external task, as expected, the DMN failed to activate in persons on the spectrum (reviewed by Stigler, McDonald, Anand, Saykin, & McDougle, 2011). This suggested that mind wandering and introspection did not take place as strongly in ASD individuals when their minds were free from external tasks.

Further studies provided compelling evidence that the DMN and theory of mind regions of autistic and neurotypical brains develop differently during passage from early childhood into the adult. The frontal lobe, which contains theory of mind circuits, is smaller in autistic children at birth; however, the autistic frontal lobe grows more rapidly after birth. This accelerated growth may cause neurons within the frontal lobe to be overconnected with one another, leading to disorganized frontal lobe function (reviewed by Courchesne & Pierce, 2005). However, connections to other parts of the brain are decreased, leading to long-range disconnection of these regions, which may impair sharing of information within the autistic brain. Many of these new findings came from measurement of a brain property called functional connectivity (FC). Two brain regions are said to connect functionally when they exhibit synchronous fMRI activity, that is, when fMRI shows they are active at the same time. FC between distant regions of the DMN was reduced in autism patients, consistent with impaired long range sharing of information. Significantly, FC was reduced more greatly as the severity of the deficit in social and communication skills increased (Assaf et al., 2010). Short range FC was, however, enhanced.

Yet another technique, Diffusion Tensor Imaging (DTI), confirmed altered development of the autistic brain. DTI measures the diffusion of water molecules in the brain's grey matter, where nerve fibers are grouped in parallel bundles that restrict water diffusion (Alexander, Lee, Lazar, & Field, 2007). DTI confirmed decreased connectivity (Travers et al., 2012), in particular connectivity for the fibers that link distant regions of the social and emotional brain (Ameis & Catani, 2015). Decreased communication between regions of the social brain caused by abnormal development is proposed to impair sharing information about social cues. This makes it difficult for people on the spectrum to understand the social behavior and emotions of others. The reason why the autistic brain develops differently is not known, but gene mutations are likely to play a role (Ziats & Rennart, 2016).

The changes in theory of mind and introspection and self-understanding in ASD involve some of the most complex functions of the brain, functions that pertain to mental state, social intuition, emotion and consciousness. Understanding these changes will surely help us bridge the gap between the ASD person and the neurotypical, accelerate diagnosis, and lead to new-targeted forms of neuropharmacology and more effective methods of therapy and education.

In addition to differences in theory of mind, 85% of people with ASD are estimated to have alexithymia type II (Rieffe, Meerum Terwogt, & Kotronopoulou, 2006), which is defined by a difficulty in

XIII. Future ("Futuro")

40 cm x 50 cm – acrylic paint, 2014

"***Future*** – it is like an unknown forest, filled with mysterious beings, but its background is bright and joyful. The colors are as cozy as a room full of toys, a small aromatic garden, or a fluttery dress during summer, feminine and romantic. The darker markings come on top, as if they were the consciousness of the pain that also accompanies life." ECK

"I wanted to show that the future is fantastic." Cacá Silva

understanding, describing, and categorizing one's own emotions, even when they are present and intense. For instance, a person might not know if they feel guilty or disappointed by someone, if they are scared or ashamed, or why are they crying or feeling anger. It is extremely important to appreciate this, as it disproves the myth that autistic people are cold and incapable of bonding with others. On the contrary, they actually get attached to people, want to help and please others, and suffer along with them (Ryndak, Downing, Jacqueline, & Morrison, 1995; Staub, Schwartz, Galluci, & Peck,, 1994), but might not be able to process what they perceive cognitively, or to categorize and infer the nature of both their own and other people's feelings. This causes perplexity, confusion, and a high level of anxiety (Capriola, Maddox, & White, 2016; Milosavljevic et al., 2016), inducing them to flight reactions, panic, aggressiveness, and self-harm. It also creates an apparent indifference. These reactions then cause misunderstandings and stress in other people, resulting in a vicious cycle of mutual frustration.

Both characteristics, systematization on one hand, and theory of mind/empathy deficit and alexithymia on the other, strongly predispose persons on the spectrum to isolated activities centered on objects that can be sorted and classified. Thus, many people on the spectrum report great pleasure and anxiety reduction when their time is devoted to their particular interests. While for many people the process of training, testing and acquiring expertise in a certain area can be an exhausting sacrifice only endured in the name of a final result, for someone on the spectrum this process is a reward in itself, which allows them to practice intensely, leading to proficiency and unexpected discovery.

In addition, having only limited access to the emotions and prospects of other people may make possible creative thinking and novel perceptions by a person on the spectrum that are not restricted by the conventional rules and beliefs of society. When someone's mind is not limited to what is perceived by society as adequate, beautiful, or acceptable, it can engage in new and unprecedented experimentation.

XIV. Spring ("Primavera") 50 cm x 60 cm– colored glue and acrylic paint, 2011

"Spring is delightful. It is feminine, delicate, tender, sweet, and also very lively and expressive. The composition is very harmonic, almost symmetrical, but despite that, the artist's unruly and daring aspects are still present. The irregular lines are a captivating aspect. Their fragility is enchanting for being clearly made with human hands that work freely, without rulers, compasses, or measuring. The painting is an invitation to be immersed in this scenery full of hope. Are they only flowers or also butterflies?" ECK

"When I think of art I think of beauty. Beauty is the mystery of life. It is not just in the eye. It is in the mind. It is our positive response to life." Agnes Martin

5. A New View: Seeing Talents and Opportunities for Integration – Art, Intelligence and Creativity

Music and painting: two welcoming refuges

The arts may have a special appeal to people on the spectrum, and their difficulties may explain why music and painting or drawing are the areas where their talents most frequently thrive. Both music and painting are forms of creation that are independent from verbal expression, which, for people with ASD, often presents itself as a confusing and puzzling code and is therefore an obstacle. Even for those whose cognition and mastery of formal language are intact, daily verbal communication is a challenge, as it includes unpredictability and a lack of clear rules. For example, intonation of speech is very telling emotionally and its appreciation is fundamental to the comprehension of a verbal message. However, these qualities of speech intonation cannot be fully explained by simple rules, and they are only perceived intuitively. Figurative language also transcends the rules of meaning, and requires linguistic flexibility and creativity to be formulated and understood. In the absence of these abilities, it is hard to understand the meaning of sentences such as "I'm on fire today"; "I've already read that a billion times"; "he kicked the bucket"; "you are such a doormat".

On the other hand, although music allows for an infinite number of possible combinations, music also follows explicit rules, and therefore music can be learned by appreciating patterns of melody and rhythm. For these reasons, the general properties of a piece of music are predictable, and it is not necessary to understand all of the individual components to grasp the general construct. This is in contrast to verbal language, where the misunderstanding of a single word or phrase can prevent the understanding of a whole sentence. As already mentioned in Chapter 4 in our discussion of the Empathizing–Systemizing Theory, it seems that people on the autism spectrum not only need implicit rules that allow for generalization, but actually have a special talent for finding them. In this context, music is a systemized universe, while spoken language is not. This difference could eventually explain an impressive paradox, which is the ease people with ASD have in interpreting the emotional undertones of music (sad, happy, scary), but not of spoken phrases.

Painting can also open a window for communication and self-expression, but in a different way. If there are any ambiguous or hidden meanings in a picture, they do not cause anxiety for the autistic person, because a picture can be interpreted in many ways and all of them are allowed. A picture can also be ignored. There is no problem in not understanding the message it supposedly conveys. In addition, the act of painting provides people with ASD the opportunity to think about and work with fascinating objects, such as when they reproduce complex patterns and abstract shapes, or consider varied placement of light sources, movement, or different perspectives of the same object, or visual details, such as in the architecture of buildings. Just like music, painting provides a universe of its own. Even when a painting has a representational nature, it does not necessarily portray objects realistically. Nor does it need to conform to social expectations to be intelligible in the way verbal expression does.

Effectiveness of music and painting: because the autistic mind perceives a different world

Superior perception and memory skills probably also contribute to the appeal of music and painting for people with ASD. For example, when it comes to music, they frequently exhibit superior tonal memory in reproducing sounds they have heard previously, and in their sense of absolute pitch, which is the ability to identify a particular tone of any audio frequency (Heaton, 2009).

When it comes to painting, people with ASD tend to focus more on the details and on the individual parts instead of on the whole, which is a great advantage in tasks that require ignoring the global picture, solving optical illusions, and seeing lines as they actually are presented. The Enhanced Perceptual Functioning Theory proposes that for people with ASD, the bias of perception for local processing is due to a superior awareness on its most basic levels (Mottron, Dawson, Soulières, Hubert, & Burack, 2006). For most people, to perceive something that is seen, the brain interprets and rearranges the stimuli it receives and presents them as a coherent and plausible whole to the mind. This does not seem to happen with people with ASD, for whom images are captured and presented to the mind in their most raw and unprocessed form. For example, when looking at a picture of two children going inside a church, most people tend to focus on the children and quickly extract the elements of the environment. They perceive that the children are moving and recognize the building as a church based on previous experiences, which are sufficient for them to interpret the situation. The goal of perception is primarily to obtain information to guide us in the world. Quick thinking and the ability to condense information are necessary, and our prior knowledge directs us to ignore details that may be considered irrelevant. In contrast, a person with ASD might focus on the lines and light constituting one of the sidewalls of the church. This would impair an overall comprehension of the setting, but could enable the identification of many other elements that

XV. Ice ("Gelo") 30 cm x 40 cm – acrylic filler, colored glue, and acrylic paint, 2012

"I have no fears about making changes, destroying the image, etc., because the painting has a life of its own."
Jackson Pollock

are usually ignored. Instead of synthesizing information and seeing a church, a person with autism would deconstruct the picture, and pay attention to details.

Directing attention to a part of the whole and being sharp-eyed are characteristics common to savant artists and their realistic drawings, as is the case with Stephen Wiltshire[1]. This artistic quality can also be found in the work of many non-savant autistic painters, and even in the work of non-autistic painters who are skilled at realistic pictorial reproduction. This clearly suggests that a bias for local processing can be regarded not just as a disorder, but also as an advantage (Drake & Winner, 2011).

Enhanced visual and spatial memory can also be observed in some people with autism. Temple Grandin[2], the most well-known person with ASD, portrays her peculiar form of visual thinking in her books. She reports that her brain stores highly precise photographic and three-dimensional images of everything she sees, and that she is capable of turning these images around, combining them, and transforming them in her mind. These abilities have been a great benefit to her practice of making drawings of corrals and slaughterhouses that have revolutionized the treatment of livestock in the United States and worldwide (Grandin, 2011).

Besides having differences in perception in the auditory and visual spheres, people on the spectrum also experience the world in a very particular and intense way through other sensory systems. For example, a soft touch can be distressful, while a squeeze may relieve anxiety. The feeling of a specific texture while chewing or the sensing of a particular smell can be more then unpleasant, being unbearable and causing anguish.

---

[1] Stephen Wiltshire–who is on the spectrum–is a British artist born in 1974 known for his extraordinary ability of drawing a complete and precise reproduction of a landscape from memory after having only observed it briefly. In 2006, he was named by Queen Elizabeth II as a Member of the Order of the British Empire. On the same year, he founded his own gallery in London. Retrieved from http://www.stephenwiltshire.co.uk

[2] Temple Grandin has a doctoral degree in animal science from the University of Illinois and is a professor at Colorado State University. She was named by the Time magazine as one of the 100 most influential people in the world, is the author of several best-sellers about autism and is part of the Neurodiversity movement. A movie about her was released by BBC: The woman who thinks like a cow. Retrieved from http://www.templegrandin.com

Each person has his or her own spectrum: an individualized look at the choices for therapy and the importance of treating concomitant disorders

With regard to the therapeutic aspects of autism, because autism may be broadly variable between individuals, a diagnosis of ASD should not, in practice, be seen as the final word because it foresees neither the particular abilities nor the difficulties of the individual, but merely places him or her in a group and explains some of their characteristics. In order to promote talents and confront challenges, therapeutic analysis must be individualized, and for that reason it is recommended that the patient's family, caregivers, therapists, and educators always have in mind a quote by Dr. Stephen Mark Shore[3] (and he too is on the spectrum): "If you've met one person with autism, you've met one person with autism."

Comorbidity is the rule for autism, which is to say, ASD usually co-occurs with other disorders that often become a main reason for the suffering of the individual and for difficulty in adapting. For instance, 30% of children with ASD also have social anxiety, 17% have obsessive-compulsive disorder (OCD), and 15% have generalized anxiety (van Steensel, Bögels, & Perrin, 2011), while 30% exhibit diagnostic criteria that are linked to attention deficit hyperactivity disorder (ADHD) (Simonoff et al., 2008). Depression, motor tics, Tourette syndrome, intellectual disability, epilepsy, sleep disorders and constipation are also common. For this reason, issues that are unreported or not recognized must always be tracked, examined, and treated, which requires specialized monitoring by a multi-professional team. There is yet no specific medication for autism, which means that pharmacological measures cannot be employed to treat communication and socialization deficits, although medicine is often used and can greatly help with comorbidities.

In addition, these problems most often change as the ASD person progresses through the different stages of life. Each stage has its own challenges and conflicts, such as challenges of establishing independence, of care of one's self, of schooling and sexuality, and therefore, therapy should go through changes, with reestablishment of its objectives and methods according to the patient's current stage of life. The same child with ASD that needed medication and psycho-pedagogical assistance for ADHD is the teenager who needs cognitive-behavioral psychotherapy to deal with social anxiety, and, maybe the adult who will need treatment for depression.

---

[3] Dr. Stephen Mark Shore is a professor at Adelphi University's School of Education and Special Education, Garden City, NY. He is chairman emeritus of the Asperger's Association of New England and a former board member of the Autism Society of America. He is also a board member of Asperger Syndrome & High Functioning Autism Association, of the Autism Services Association, and of other associations related to the autism spectrum. Retrieved from http://www.usautism.org/who_are_you_autism.html

XVI. Beauty ("A linda") 50 cm x 70 cm – colored glue, acrylic filler, and acrylic paint, 2012

"There is no must in art because art is free." Wassily Kandinsky

"It shows beauty." Cacá Silva

The multiplicity of approaches offered for the treatment of ASD is bewildering and often brings the challenge of selecting between verified effective methods and experimental methods, or methods under evaluation or even suggestions that seem absurd. The challenge is even greater when considering that results obtained with a specific autistic group are not necessarily replicable with others, as severity of symptoms, the degree of intellectual disability, the degree of verbal communication impairment, the presence of concomitant disorders, age, etc. are factors that greatly affect the response to a therapeutic approach. In addition, despite the fact that some methods are systemized, their application is subject to variation, as the interaction between patient and therapist will always be unique. Conditions of treatment also vary, such as the environment in which the intervention is provided (a university health center, a private clinic, a school), the professional involved (a researcher, a private professional, an educator, the parents), and also the duration and intensity of the intervention. An additional consideration is that most studies have positive short-term results, meaning that the studies report some weeks of improvement, but they do not verify that these changes are maintained afterwards. It is fundamental to be aware of these limitations, as it is important to know there is not one particular method that has been proven to be effective for all people with ASD. This leads to the premise that individual analysis is of vital importance and is the most important factor when choosing a therapeutic method. In light of this, what follows are general directions to guide caregivers on the major intervention methods.

First, it is important to know that autism does not have a cure, and therefore any treatment promising that should be taken skeptically. Moreover, the first priority of the treatment has to be to ensure quality of life for the person with ASD, including the person's independence, social functioning, capacity for communication, and, above everything else, satisfaction with life and with oneself. Therefore, the aim is not to "normalize" the child and abolish all behaviors that distinguish him or her from others, but to recognize the aspects of the child that can be strengthened and the barriers that can be overcome, while still respecting his or her limits. For example, eye contact can be encouraged, but is important to know that eye contact requires an arduous effort for a person on the spectrum. Many spectrum people report they cannot concentrate on what they hear or on what they intend to express if they have to make eye contact, and others say it bothers and disturbs them to the point of being physically painful. For this reason, although lack of eye contact may seem strange to others, the comfort of the person with ASD during a social interaction should be given priority.

A second example is repetitive motion, such as rocking the body or head, flapping the arms, and making vocalizations, which can be embarrassing, but are described by people with ASD as a need that allows them to relieve tension and reduce fear, block unpleasant stimuli (such as excessive noise, people, light, or requests), or simply express happiness. Thus, an individual analysis that tries to understand the particular situation of the person on the spectrum, including why the person is carrying out this or that body language, plus the acceptance of this form of expression are preferred to forcedly repressing these behaviors. It is crucial to have spaces and moments in which the person with ASD can use their own strategies of coping and balance.

It is clear that we must protect him or her from self-harmful behavior, but it is worth noting that interpreting every behavior is essential and should precede the choice of method of intervention. Thus, taking into account that moments of uncontrollable and seemingly random psychomotor agitation can usually be traced to specific causes such as excessive therapy, a change in routine, fear, and frustration, it is recommended that the therapist develop enough sensitivity to notice the first signs of emotional overload and then to ensure "psychological decompression" so that these incidents can be prevented. Breaks and moments of isolation are important, as they are moments of freedom, of peace, and of being oneself with no obligations toward the narrow idea of achieving socially desirable normality.

For didactic purposes, and with no intention of making a complete list, ASD therapeutic methods can be divided into 1) intensive behavioral intervention (such as Applied Behavioral *Analysis* (ABA), developed by Ole Ivar Lovaas, *Pivotal Response Training*, developed by Robert and Lynn Kogel, or *Early Start Denver Model*, developed by Sally Rogers and Geraldine Dawson); 2) relationship-based intervention (such as *Floortime*, developed by Stanley Greenspan and Serena Wieder); 3) alternative communication methods; 4) socioemotional training; 5) cognitive behavioral therapy; 6) sensory integration therapy; 7) animal-assisted therapy; and 8) interventions based on artistic expression (such as art therapy and music therapy).

Adjusting behavior versus building relationships: the importance of early treatment and the controversy over ABA

Programs based on ABA are focused on behavior adaptation: adequate behavior is rewarded with preestablished prizes, and inadequate behavior is redirected or altered. Instructions are always simple and precise, and rules are clear. Parents usually collaborate so that this therapy can be carried out in the family's home environment, resulting in 30 to 40 hours of therapy in a week. The child's responses are molded through intensive repetition, resulting in improvement of communication and social adaptation (Smith & Eikeseth, 2011).

Pivotal Response Training is based on the principles of ABA, but with a more naturalistic approach, involving the child's interests and a natural environment (Koegel et al., 1989). Some basic abilities are taught, such as how to form appropriate responses to multiple clues, self-control, motivation, and the initiative for increased social interaction, all with the intention of providing a general training that can be applied to different situations. Generally, there is behavioral improvement, even for those behaviors that are not specifically approached, and the parents are greatly involved in the entire process.

The Early Start Denver Model is an intervention focused on relationships, but also based on the principles of ABA. Its main characteristics are applicability during the early phases of development, such as between 12 and 18 months of age (Rogers & Dawson, 2010). It focuses on affective interaction with the learning

XVII. Circle of Polka Dots ("Ciclo de Bolinhas") 50 cm x 70 cm – acrylic paint, 2014.

"My art originates from hallucinations only I can see. I translate the hallucinations and obsessional images that plague me into sculptures and paintings." Yayoi Kusama of communication in the context of relationship experiences, and with attention to the child's developmental phases. It also employs naturalistic behavior strategies, which means that the strategies are based on daily situations and natural environments, so sessions can take place at home. It also employs playful activities and intense parental participation.

In general, there is clear evidence that children who receive at an early age (before the child is 4 years old), structured treatment based on ABA that is intensive (more than 15 hours per week) and that is implemented for a long period of time (between 8 months and 2 years) exhibit significant improvement in language, cognition, and social functioning. Nevertheless, these results vary greatly, and the factors that allow for a better response to the intervention are still unclear (Weitlauf et al., 2014).

Nonetheless, ABA is controversial. Despite having the support of a great part of the medical and scientific communities, self-help groups and societies that defend the rights of people with ASD strongly criticize and reject this treatment. The main objections are that ABA is founded on a negative notion of ASD that regards it to be a group of disabilities that must be eliminated, and it is based on procedures employed in animal conditioning experiments (desired behavior is induced through rewards while undesired behavior is erased). In addition, in the case of ABA, there is no attempt to understand what is happening to the child and to his or her perceptions and emotions. The objective is behavioral adaptation so that the child can become as close as possible to what is considered a normal child, ignoring the fact that each child is and will always be different. In this view, ABA compromises self-esteem and self-acceptance by teaching the child to deny, suppress and hide many of the traits that are part of them. Finally, ABA may underestimate children with ASD, especially those with limited verbal communication abilities.

A well-known and memorable example is the story of Ido Kedar[4], a young American who at 16 published the book *Ido in Autismland* (2012), in which he discloses his autobiography and criticizes the treatments he had received. As he has severe autistic symptoms, being incapable of communicating verbally and incapable of following his therapists' motor commands, he was underestimated and misunderstood during the many years he went through 40 hours of ABA sessions weekly. His life was drastically transformed when he managed to express himself and finally demonstrate his intelligence, critical ability, and humor through an iPad app. He radically rejects the ABA method and relates in detail how torturing it was to live with his mind stuck in his body, to be treated as a baby, and to have to point at pictures or touch his own nose without being able to express himself much beyond that level. His mistakes were meticulously annotated and interpreted as proof of deficits in comprehension and intellect, forcing him to train repeatedly on the same tasks with no apparent progress.

---

[4] Retrieved from http://idoinautismland.blogspot.com.br

Floortime is an intervention centered on the child and the child's interests. It is less directed, which is to say that the child has more freedom to guide the activities and to interact with the therapist during the sessions. The therapist tries to get closer to the child's particular universe, always starting with what is most appealing to the child and slowly introducing more elaborate and complex stimuli, which expand processing, emotional control, empathy, shared attention, and socialization skills. The approach strategies are always flexible, spontaneous and improvised, including music, games, dialogue, and toys (Greenspan & Wieder, 2006).

Verbal and alternative communication

It is estimated that around 30% of children of school age with ASD have no verbal communication ability (Tager-Flusberg, Paul, & Lord, 2005), which is a serious problem as it is linked to worsened cognitive, social, familial, and psychological performance. Nonverbal children are usually misunderstood and underestimated, as was already addressed in Chapter 5 (Adjusting behavior versus building relationships: the importance of early treatment and the controversy over ABA) through Ido Kedar's dramatic example.

In reality, these children form a quite heterogeneous group that is still not very well studied. For example, recent data show that the assumption that verbal expression deficit is always accompanied by intellectual and vocabulary deficit is incorrect. Many nonverbal children do in fact have an intellectual deficit, but many others do not. The same applies to receptive language ability, which may or may not be impaired (Munson et al., 2008; Rapin, Dunn, Allen, Stevens, & Fein, 2009).

In 2004, the American government, through the Interagency Autism Coordinating Committee (IACC)[5], set as a long-term goal that 90% of children with ASD will have acquired functional verbal language at age 5. This implies identification of children in need and intervention at an early age. However, the means for achieving this level of verbal proficiency has still not been established. Intensive behavioral training based on verbal instructions yields verifiable results, even if the results vary widely from case to case. Augmentative and alternative communication training has also been widely encouraged and involves many nonverbal resources for expressive and receptive communication, and employs both digital and nondigital

---

[5] The Interagency Autism Coordinating Committee (IACC) is a Federal advisory committee that coordinates all efforts within the Department of Health and Human Services (HHS) concerning autism spectrum disorder (ASD). It also provides advice to the Secretary of Health and Human Services regarding Federal activities related to autism spectrum disorder. Retrieved from http://www.iacc.hhs.gov

XVIII. Butterfly ("Borboleta") 40 cm x 50 cm – acrylic paint, 2013

"***Crazy***, psychedelic, and shockingly happy butterfly. A butterfly that does not ask for permission to fly." ECK media. In verbal instruction training, we have sign language, communication boards with pictures, letters, or other symbols. The Picture Exchange Communication System (PECS) is a very well known example and consists of cards with pictures that the child points at to communicate. Among the electronic resources are apps for the iPad and other tablets, some with voice digitalization systems, such as Proloquo2Go[6], which can convert clicked images into requests and words that describe feelings, objects, or places. Alternative communication has the advantage of using visual information, to which people with ASD are extremely receptive, and, therefore, the child receives stimuli that are pleasant and appealing to them. Many children, fascinated by the pictures and by handling the iPad, are more easily led away from their isolation and are motivated to express themselves, to participate in communication games with other people, and to learn social and academic skills. For these reasons, this resource has become popular in schools.

There is no empirical evidence supporting the fear that alternative communication could inhibit the development of verbal communication. On the contrary, study results indicate that there is in fact a facilitating element to alternative communication, specifically, that children stimulated by alternative communication visual resources exhibit a higher linguistic development than those who have received only verbal stimuli. For example, Kasari et al. (2014) demonstrated in a study with 61 nonverbal school-age children (5 to 8 years) that those who had a voice digitalization system in conjunction to behavioral intervention with verbal instructions exhibited better language expression development when compared to the children who had only behavioral intervention. In a different study, Schreibman and Stahmer (2014) evaluated 39 nonverbal children between 20 and 45 months old, for a period of six months, by comparing the effects of Pivotal Response Training, which involves verbal stimulation, to the effects of PECS. Both methods were equally efficient and led to significant improvement in many aspects of communication. On average, children acquired 80 spoken words, and 78% of them managed to acquire at least 10 words. The authors comment that, despite the results being positive and overall encouraging, individual variability was too great; therefore, it was not possible to identify which child profile had a better response with which methods and thus the means for selecting the best method is still a matter of study.

Cognitive behavioral therapy

As previously mentioned, people with ASD must cope not only with the symptoms connected to autism itself, but also with other problems, such as depression and anxiety. These problems could possibly result from difficulties in social interaction and from experiences of social rejection and from lack of

[6] Retrieved from http://www.assistiveware.com/product/proloquo2go

understanding by others, all of which are frequent in the spectrum. Moreover, these problems also result in the worsening of the very issues that caused them, as they lead to isolation, avoidance, fear, pessimism, and lack of motivation, giving rise to an unfortunate self-perpetuating cycle, with the lowering of self-esteem, quality of life, and self-satisfaction. In this context, the linkage of training in social skills (which will be addressed later on this chapter, in *Adolescence and adult life: socialization, socioemotional abilities training, and sexuality*) to cognitive behavioral therapy could be very helpful.

Cognitive behavioral therapy is an already well-established and widely used approach for a great variety of psychiatric disorders. It is based on the principle that we can change our emotions and behaviors if we transform our perceptions and beliefs. Thus, cognitive restructuring involves confrontation between the patient and his or her way of thinking about, and of perceiving the world, which at the start can be excessively negative, fatalistic, radical, inflexible, or self-centered. During the behavioral therapy sessions, the patient's interpretations of reality are discussed with the therapist in a logical light that reveals their distorted aspects. For example, sadness can arise from unfounded generalizations (he does not like me, and, consequently, no one else does) or from inwardly turning, egocentric perceptions (everyone is against me). Social anxiety can result from the belief that one is incapable and inferior, or from the belief that one cannot commit a single mistake if one is to be accepted by a group.

The behavioral element of this strategy includes facilitating changes in behavior by, for example, writing down all negative thoughts and bringing the notes to therapy, altering harmful routines or habits (eating, sleeping, socializing, self-expression, behavior when faced with stressful situations), or, in the case of exposure therapy, exposing the person to situations that may cause fear or apprehension and practicing coping strategies that are learned during the sessions. The process in general is gradual and, if necessary, the therapist may be present at the moment the person is exposed to difficult situations.

Behavioral Interventions for Anxiety in Children with Autism (BIACA), developed by Jeff Wood and collaborators (2009) in the University of California, is a type of cognitive behavioral therapy adapted to children with ASD that focuses especially on anxiety disorders, OCD, social ability, and on working with parents. It provides very substantial results, and its place in the therapeutic armory is very well established (Weitlauf et al., 2014). However, it is important to note that it has some limitations arising from the fact that this method requires cognitive abilities for self-criticism and abstraction that are sufficiently preserved and also adequate verbal communication abilities, because this intervention is strongly based on dialogues with the therapist.

Sensory processing and sensory integration therapy

It is estimated that 90% of children with ASD exhibit some alteration of sensory processing (Leekam,

XIX. Labyrinth ("Labirinto")

50 cm x 70 cm – acrylic paint, 2013

"In art there is only one thing that counts; the thing you can't explain. Art is meant to disturb, science reassures."
Georges Braque

"I thought about the movie *Pan's Labyrinth*." Cacá Silva

Nieto, Libby, Wing, & Gould, 2007), which can manifest in an individual as hypersensitivity to common stimuli (such as noises, lights, smells, and textures) and low susceptibility to relevant stimuli such as unresponsiveness to pain or to the child's own name. While more serious during childhood, these alterations are common to all age groups with ASD.

Ornitz (1974) proposed that sensory alterations could be associated with some repetitive and stereotyped forms of behavior that can be, at times, attempts at self-stimulation and, at other times, attempts at self-reassurance, creating a shield against unpleasant stimuli. Self-stimulation may also take place in the form of sensory preferences or even sensory cravings in pursuit of certain stimuli–such as palpating objects of a specific texture or in a specific way.

Hypersensitivity in particular can be very disturbing and cause anxiety, phobias, social avoidance, rejection of food, and episodes of psychomotor agitation, especially in children with language deficits who cannot explain what is causing their stress. Some people with ASD wear earplugs and sunglasses as protection against unpleasant stimuli.

Sensory Integration Therapy consists of offering simultaneous stimuli via different sense channels, such as tactile, proprioceptive (sensing the position of the body or parts of the body in space), and vestibular, through playful activities. For instance, it creates challenging situations by using swings, hammocks, rolls, balance platforms, or balls, requiring adaptive responses from the nervous system, which induces progressive changes in the integration of information. Sensory Integration Therapy is an evolving and dynamic process that is always centered on the child and based on the difficulties and needs of the individual. This form of therapy is highly flexible and interactive, that is, it can be adjusted depending on the child's reactions and behavior, and it requires active participation. The goals can be to reduce avoidance and defensive behavior (such as not wanting to take showers or not tolerating certain environments), anxiety, self-stimulation and hyperactivity. It seeks to improve motor coordination, and may improve socialization and communication skills, because the relationship with the therapist has a vital role as the therapy proceeds. Various studies confirm the effectiveness of this approach (Case-Smith, Weaver, & Fristad, 2015).

Sensory Integration Therapy should not be mistaken for sensory-based interventions, which consist of passive stimulation strategies to alleviate anxiety, such as massage, friction, rocking, repetitive movements, and wearing clothes with weights.

Animal-assisted therapy

Animal-assisted therapies (AAT) are interventions performed by a licensed therapist in which an animal has a central role. Animal-assisted activities do not require the presence of a therapist; hence, these playful and recreational opportunities are more spontaneous and less methodic.

A large number of reports testify to the positive effects of animals on people with ASD, especially on socioemotional behavior. Animals reduce the stress, anxiety, and isolation of people with ASD and improve their socialization and their initiative to communicate and interact with their families. The causes of those benefits are still not understood, although some possible reasons are the fact that animals are less demanding and more predictable than humans; furthermore, animals provide a rich variety of sensory stimulations and do not interact verbally.

An Australian study by O'Haire, McKenzie, McCune, and Slaughter (2014) demonstrated that the mere presence of a guinea pig in a classroom had remarkable effects on school-age children. They monitored 64 children with ASD between 5 and 13 years old from 15 different schools. Twice a week during eight weeks, the child with ASD participated, along with two other children from his or her class and an untrained adult, in a 20-minute session of activities with the animal. They could touch, pet, brush, bath, feed, take pictures, prepare the food, clean the cage, build toys, and make a circle inside which the animal would move. Parents and teachers noticed an improvement in social interaction; children also showed higher motivation to go to school and reduction in avoidance behavior. At the end of the study, half the animals stayed in the classrooms and the parents of participant children adopted the other half.

Among all animal-assisted therapies, equine-assisted therapy is probably the most promising option for people with ASD. It incorporates different modalities and protocols that can include occupational therapists, speech therapists, and psychologists, along with the equine-therapist. In addition to riding, it involves horse-care and feeding activities, and playtime with the animal. This therapy improves socialization and emotional response; furthermore, the rhythmic movement of the horse improves motor skills, since it stimulates balance, posture correction, and motor coordination. A study by Borgi et al. (2016) monitored 15 children with ASD, between 6 and 12 years old, who participated in a 6-month program of equine-assisted therapy that consisted of 25 sessions, 60-70 minutes each. During each class, the children learned about horse anatomy and behavior, how to take care of the animal, and how to saddle it. Afterwards, they led the horse to a pasture and went for a ride. There were posters with drawings containing visual instructions on the walls. Compared to the control group of thirteen children from the waiting list–who did not receive any other treatment–the participants had a significant improvement in social and motor skills, and a reduction in the time needed to solve a problem.

Music and art therapy: breaking the shell and finding the pearl

Traditionally, therapies for persons on the autism spectrum focus on behavioral adaptations that strengthen appropriate behaviors with preestablished rewards, and that modify or alter inadequate ones. The procedures are straightforward and precise and the rules for carrying them out are clear. To complement these approaches, there are additional types of therapy that consider subjective expression and the link formed with the therapist as major factors that make possible change.

XX. Time ("Tempo")

50 cm x 50 cm – acrylic on canvas, 2014

"***Time*** – time is not a straight line, time is not a uniform measure, and time stretches, distorts, and expands itself. Time is a personal experience that is expressed by colors. It even seems to resemble a work of quantum physics, but it is art capturing the infinite." ECK

"*... because time doesn't stop*." Cacá Silva

In art therapy, art is used to enable people to overcome their social, emotional, or cognitive difficulties. The objective is not the final artistic product and the therapy is not concerned with artistic education. The focus is on the art-related processes of each session. Primarily, this therapy offers a safe, predictable, and organized space where the patient can chose a preferred form of expression, free from the need for verbal communication and free from judgments of right or wrong and free from judgments of adequate or inadequate, or of logical or incoherent. This allows the patient to get in touch with his or her feelings in a nonintellectual, more intuitive way that does not search for answers, an approach that reduces fear and anxiety. The therapist intervenes indirectly, through suggested or available activities and materials. Eventually, the therapist can verbalize what takes place during the therapy, and can participate in the therapy's creative activity or cooperative game, or he or she can simply provide a supportive presence. A trustworthy relationship is built up through artistic activity, which is an element that both the therapist and the patient share. There are various art technics that can be employed, such as collage, clay work, and painting.

Art as an occupation can minimize the fixation of children on stereotyped behaviors and, taking into account the fact that the creative process demands preparation, planning, and focus, art can also help them organize themselves mentally, especially when they exhibit hyperactive behavior. Some important and significant steps are to choose carefully the materials they will use, the place where they will work, tool placement, the manner in which they will work, and their objectives. Having in the end a concrete result–the piece of art–empowers people with ASD with the pleasant experience of an activity that is both structured and that has a goal.

Art therapy can also help children overcome hypersensitivity or the avoidance of materials or situations, such as getting children used to tolerating glue, clay, or papier-mâché on their fingers, and sharing a space with other people, among others.

In music therapy, the therapist establishes a dialogue with the child through music. As in art therapy, various methods are possible, that is, individual or group work; singing; melody; rhythms; improvisation, and imitation. Music therapy is a unique tool for people with ASD, as it takes advantage of their affinity for music and their natural musical talent. The mere act of listening to music helps children with ASD to calm down and to adapt to new tasks and spaces. Music improves motor coordination and attention; reduces hyperactivity and repetitive movements, and above all, opens a new path to verbal communication and socialization.

It is commonly accepted that verbal language, empathy, and the theory of mind develop from imitation, that is to say, from a process in which the baby visually perceives someone's gesturing, mimicking, or speech, and represents it in motor areas of his or her own brain. The discovery of mirror neurons complemented and supported this idea. These cells form a neural network that is activated either when someone performs an action or observes someone else performing that same action. This "mirroring" is probably the basis of our ability to comprehend the intention behind the gestures of another person. Considering this possibility, Ramachandran and Oberman (Dapretto et al., 2006) proposed the Broken Mirrors Theory, which postulates that many deficits associated with the autism spectrum are due to a dysfunction of the Mirror Neuron system. In this context, music seems to be the ideal activity to activate mirror neurons (Wan, Demaine, Zipse, Norton, & Schlaug, 2010), as it involves observing other people, various interactive games, reciprocity, and imitation, such as playing the same melody on different instruments, following or responding to a rhythm, and completing a song. These elements require shared attention and intentional communication, which create a bridge to the acquisition of verbal expression (Andrade & Konkiewitz, 2011).

Aside from activating areas of the brain traditionally associated with language, motor skills, and spatial abilities, music also activates subcortical areas related to affective processing, and it is capable of evoking emotions spontaneously in the absence of external associations. For this reason, refined music is particularly efficient in resonating with our basic emotional systems through ancient neural circuits established by our genes–many of which we share with other mammals. Therefore, our love for music probably reflects the ancestral ability of our mammalian brain to transmit and receive basic emotional sounds that awaken feelings. People with ASD have clearly preserved this ability, despite all their difficulties with affective processing (Allen, Hill & Heaton, 2009; Heaton & Allen, 2009).

Adolescence and adult life: socialization, socioemotional abilities training, and sexuality

During childhood, the life of a child with ASD is centered around school, therapies, and recreational activities, whereas in adolescence, especially after finishing elementary or high school, this focus is no longer available and his or her life may be led into a world of emptiness. The near absence of structures that encourage professionalization and socialization leads to a life of loneliness, inertia, and lack of meaning. Some achievements that took great effort and dedication to be accomplished during childhood and adolescence may be lost altogether during adulthood, and the risk of developing mental health disorders such as depression and anxiety increases. A recent study (Gotham et al., 2015) showed that even in a group of 255 high-functioning autism people (i.e., with intellectual level equal to or greater than average), 42% had a college degree; only 25% worked a full time job; half reported discrimination at work; 76% had anxiety disorder; 75%, depression, and 40%, ADHD.

Autism is traditionally associated with low interest in social interaction and with an incapacity for intimate interactions–romantic bonds included. Nonetheless, this characterization does not include all possibilities, and hence it is a shortsighted and prejudiced view. The need to be among others and to share interests is variable and depends on countless factors, such as intelligence, extent of verbal language development, concomitant disorders, level of autism severity, and previous socialization experiences.

XXI. Sunset ("Pôr do Sol")

30 cm x 40 cm – acrylic paint, 2012

"The ***sunset*** looks like a revelation, a miracle! It is as if the sun emerged amidst a dark night. We do not see a soft and warm transition between day and night; on the contrary, it is the encounter between orange and yellow with deep blue, which creates an apocalyptical and surreal view. The variations of blue intensity and the free brushstrokes in different directions create movement and turn night into something shadier and stormier." ECK

"I was inspired by the sunset actually." Cacá Silva

It is important to know that having autism does not necessarily entail a desire to be isolated. On the contrary, many people with ASD do want to socialize, but they are hindered by socioemotional difficulties; that is to say, they struggle to interpret social rules, subtlety of language and nonverbal signs such as facial expression, gesture, and intonation. Most of us learn implicitly how to start a conversation, how to choose a subject of common interest, when to let the other person speak and when to answer, how to be clear and concise without saying irrelevant and uninteresting details, and how to contradict someone without being offensive. However, people with ASD may need explicit training and orientation to learn those abilities.

There are different training methodologies available, especially in English, such as Social Stories[7], which exemplifies everyday situations of interaction. They are displayed on posters or specific digital platforms, but people can also watch them on videos, or with programs such as the Superheroes Social Skills[8] program, which uses animated videos and other resources including games, cards, and comics. Another possibility is to use virtual reality such as Second Life™, which offers different environments (e.g., in an office, a diner, a store, and a park) which people can visit using an avatar. Kandalaft, Didehbani, and Krawczyk (2013) adapted this technology, creating a safe space in Second Life™ to be used as a training environment for situations such as meeting new people, having a job interview, and making financial decisions. The patient interacts with the virtual character of another player–who is actually a therapist. The objective is to improve emotion recognition, theory of mind, and conversational skills. Although it was a pilot experiment with only eight participants, the results after ten sessions were significant and long-term.

Training can also be done in groups, with dramatization techniques in which the employment of different roles allows the person to develop different perspectives and to improve empathy and theory of mind. In a safe therapeutic context, the patient can be recorded so he or she can later watch and analyze his or her social performance. By watching him or herself in the recording, the patient can better understand the therapeutic observations made by the therapist.

Be it individual or group training, it is essential for the training to be based on previous individual evaluation. The therapist needs to know the patient's profile of difficulties, level of cognitive development, interests, and talents to establish specific goals and to choose the most appropriate medium, such as visual information, multimedia, games, or music. Sessions must be well structured and predictable; language must be simple and direct. The objectives must be clear to the patient.

---

[7] Retrieved from http://www.educateautism.com/social-stories.html

[8] Retrieved from https://pacificnwpublish.com/products/Superheroes-Social-Skills%3A-A-Multimedia-Program.html

A common problem faced by people with ASD is a difficulty in generalization and transfer of acquired knowledge from a specific context to another slightly different one; hence, the training requires practicing various situations.

Sexuality within the autism spectrum is as complex and diverse as for people not on the spectrum, as it is more than just a biological impulse. Sexuality determines both the image that a person has of him or herself and the position that this person occupies inside a group, and involves central existential purposes such as creating lasting bonds, family ties, and having offspring. It also encompasses moral, religious, and cultural issues. Sexual welfare includes knowledge, thoughts and feelings toward sex, self-image, relationship with one's own body, self-expression, and interaction with a partner.

Sexual behavior of people on the spectrum is often described as egocentric and inappropriate, with masturbation during improper situations, excessive self-stimulation (which could cause injuries), and exhibitionism. However, this view is distorted and misrepresents ASD people. Persons on the spectrum face a great variety of barriers to having a fulfilling sexual life. As people on the spectrum have difficulty communicating, social acts such as trying to flirt, approaching someone else, showing interest in someone and revealing that he or she has fallen in love all become great challenges. People on the spectrum may internalize a hurtful belief that they are asexual, undesirable, or incapable of having intimacy with someone, and hence they may be discouraged from trying to have any romantic or sexual interactions. Negative experiences during childhood and adolescence, such as rejection or bullying, may lead to isolation as a form of self-protection. Some stimuli may feel uncomfortable or too intense due to sensorial particularities, which may alter responses and excitability patterns. Nonetheless, in spite of these barriers–and contrary to common sense–people with ASD can have a high level of knowledge about sex, an active sexual life, and a long-lasting romantic relationship; they may even start a family (Byers, Nichols, & Voyer, 2013).

The internet has made all information available, so that any person with sufficient cognitive skills can obtain knowledge or clarify personal doubts, including those about sex, however this does not replace individual support. People with ASD may experience an especially disturbing transition from childhood to adolescence. Body changes and social expectations of a new behavior (independence, adult attitudes) could/might generate insecurity and fear. The changes that happen in adolescence–such as the first period, first ejaculation, breast growth, body hair growth, voice changes, and masturbation–are destabilizing factors that interrupt a stage of life and demand the establishment of a new balance and a new identity, which creates a highly vulnerable moment for people with ASD. The need for acceptance and adequacy, in addition to the need to communicate difficulties, may result in a naïve and nonassertive behavior that can turn them into easy targets for sexual assault, sexual exploitation, and unprotected sex.

It is very important to discuss and explain sex not only in its technical and biological aspects, but also in a way that allows the safe sharing of subjective experiences such as fantasies, anxieties, and frustrations. Each individual and each situation demands a different approach based on the person's intellectual development, linguistic abilities, family context, structures for social support, and religious beliefs, among other factors.

XXII. Path ("Caminho") 50 cm x 60 cm – colored glue and acrylic paint, 2013

"***Path*** – the path is colored and clear. It looks full of light, sunny, and easy to be found. However, it is closed on itself; it goes nowhere. There is no way out except for the straight golden lines that break the circle and connect the element in the center (doesn't it resemble a baby inside a womb?) to the exterior that has, coincidentally, the same purple color." ECK

"I thought about the path we go through in life, very cool." Cacá Silva

A misunderstood intelligence profile

People with ASD may be considered as having high or low-functioning autism. Nonetheless, this method of classification is currently being questioned. If we consider educational and healthcare systems, these labels probably reduce the chances of detection and treatment of cognitive difficulties for those considered high functioning. Furthermore, those classified as low functioning may be continually underestimated and receive little stimulation.

In addition, the concept of intelligence within the autism spectrum must be reviewed, as the tests that evaluate it are based on the idea that intelligence consists of a single characteristic that is uniform, measurable, and has a normal distribution among the population, or, in other words, that it is a variable just like weight, height, or blood pressure, and therefore that people can vary in quantity and in numeric value, but not in profile. This idea does not allow for the existence of different forms of intelligence (Duncan, 2005; Duncan et al., 2000; Konkiewitz, 2014). The problem is that the cognitive profile of a person with ASD and their forms of perceiving and establishing relationships are unique, hence the evaluation of their potentialities through standardized psychometric tests aimed at the general population is questionable.

In fact, the intelligence of people with autism has probably been misjudged and underestimated for decades. For example, the Wechsler Intelligence Scale for Children (WISC) is widely used in IQ tests; however, many tasks demand good verbal comprehension, which is the biggest weakness of many people with ASD. Indeed, on a test in which one must arrange cubes of different colors in certain patterns, the performance of people with ASD is above average. This discordance impairs the validity of these analysis instruments and their interpretation for this group, which indicates that the final IQ values (verbal and nonverbal IQs) do not represent the real capabilities of people with ASD.

Another well-known test is the Raven's Advanced Progressive Matrices™ (APM). The APM has advantages over the WISC as it depends less on verbal abilities, and it instead evaluates a person's capacity to infer rules from not previously known data using abstraction, logic, and deductive thinking. Two recent studies (Dawson, Soulières, Gernsbacher, & Mottron, 2007; Soulières, Dawson, Gernsbacher, & Mottron, 2011) show how the estimation of cognitive skills can vary depending on the instrument used to measure them. In the Dawson et al. study, the scores of autistic children on the WISC-III[9] were at the 26th percentile for Verbal IQ, and 31st percentile for Performance IQ (both implying mental retardation) whereas their scores on the APM were at the 56th percentile (i.e., implying an average intelligence). Furthermore, no child within the ASD group could be classified at the range of high intelligence in the WISC-III, whereas a third of this same group were in this range on the APM test (at or above the 90th percentile). These data

---

[9] The method used was the Wechsler Intelligence Scale for Children – Third Edition.

show an important, even alarming, aspect of intelligence testing in the context of ASD. Using tests that were developed for neurotypicals may not be appropriate for persons on the spectrum, and indeed our criteria for intelligence may have to be reexamined. Not considering these factors could lead to false conclusions, which could seriously affect–even devastate–a child.

If the goal is to aid a person, psychometric testing should not have the final word as it is important to consider that, along with the fact that these instruments are limited, the testing situation is artificial, for it occurs in a strange environment, within a limited amount of time, and it may cause anxiety or disinterest, all of which influence the results. The result, which supposedly reflects the degree of intelligence of a person, is questionable and says nothing about individual characteristics of cognitive processing, which are the preferential resources used to establish associations and to solve problems such as the grouping of photo-realistic images; creation of abstract patterns; deduction; generalization, and verbal, numeric, or musical thinking. It is not about describing an individual's personal interests, but rather the way someone thinks, as people with the same IQ percentile can differ immensely in mental processes and in mechanisms of attention control, capacity for persistence, maintenance of motivation, and impulse inhibition as well as cognitive flexibility, skills in different domains (linguistic, musical, imaginary), creativity, and emotional and personality traits. These differences are more accentuated and unpredictable in people with ASD, and to comprehend each person individually may be the key to understanding their minds and to optimizing their potentials. In addition, intelligence is not a static attribute. On the contrary, it develops through adequate training, as the brain is an extremely dynamic system, characterized by its neuroplasticity, which is to say its capacity to change its own functioning and anatomic structure in response to external demands (Brans et al., 2010; Konkiewitz & Andrade, 2012). Synaptic connections are truly moldable and new synapses can be established, inasmuch those processes depend on environmental stimulation and are the base to formation of knowledge and memory (Olesen, Westerberg, & Klingberg, 2004; Scholz, Klein, Behrens, & Johansen-Berg, 2009).

Integrative and systemic approaches to intelligence, such as proposed by Robert Sternberg (1985), Stephen Ceci (1996), and Howard Gardner (1999), offer concepts that better adjust to particular characteristics of the autistic mind. Regardless of their differences, these approaches recognize that intelligence is composed of various skills and cannot be reduced to a simple numerical score. Intelligence presents itself in each person with a unique profile. It is plastic, and can be modified by the environment and by experience. Intelligence unfolds from a complex interaction between the person and environment through time. Therefore, these integrative conceptions of intelligence admit the coexistence of both deficient aspects and highly functional aspects of the ASD person, traits that are typical in autism yet are hard for the neurotypical to comprehend. People with ASD are still commonly labeled as retarded due to their low performance on tasks that demand verbal communication, and comprehension of social and cultural norms; whereas their high performance in mathematics and in visual-spatial or musical tasks is seen as novel and a result of altered cerebral connections as proposed by the Weak Central Coherence Theory (WCC) (Happé & Frith, 2006).

XXIII. Happiness ("Felicidade")

50 cm x 60 cm – acrylic paint, 2014

"***Happiness*** – at first sight, it is a chaotic image with no exterior meaning. However, colors are distributed and combined in a vibrating and harmonious contrast, a recurring theme in the artist's work. In other words, the colors result in something we recognize as beautiful without knowing why. There are no lines, just colors that stumble upon each other, but do not blend. The image has this certain inquietude and turmoil. It seems like happiness is complicated, labyrinthine, and difficult to go through." ECK

"I thought that I'm happy, cheerful." Cacá Silva

Can people with ASD be creative?

Amongst all of our characteristics, creativity is probably the most genuinely human. It reflects the enchantment we can see in things, our capacity for transforming the world around us, and our sensitivity to beauty. At the same time, it is one of our less comprehensible characteristics, an unpredictable and changeable skill, one that comes to us through unknown paths. There have been many attempts to investigate creativity in a scientific way, to try to circumscribe it inside a concept. Nevertheless, all approaches, whether to consider it a trait of personality, a mental process, or a performance, clash with his or her restrictions.

Perhaps these restrictions also create cognitive barriers to the comprehension of the creative process in an autistic mind. Certainly, when we define and measure creativity, it becomes a rigid idea and no longer encompasses diversity. It is possible that people with ASD are creative in ways that these concepts do not recognize. This is because people on the spectrum are often repetitive, less flexible, intolerant to changes, and fixed in routines and rituals, qualities inconsistent with many concepts of creativity. ASD persons also exhibit difficulties in theory of mind and in make believe, and they do not create imaginary worlds, unlike creative people, who are typically eager for innovation, are in search for social interactions, and are interested in changing and recombining objects. Furthermore, people with ASD frequently present a low performance in standardized tests of divergent thinking. These tests are based on the definition of creativity as a capacity to generate a product that is both new and valuable, and considered useful and/or satisfactory. They are also based on the idea that divergent thinking (i.e., to elaborate different solutions to a single question) is its cognitive correlative. Hence, taking divergent thinking as a reflection of the creative potential of a person, test instruments that measure it were developed, such as the task of alternative uses, in which one must find different possibilities to use the same object (e.g., a brick) within a limited time. Performance is evaluated according to various criteria such as the quantity of ideas and their originality.

Undoubtedly, performance in the task of divergent thinking reflects creative potential and can predict the quantity and the quality of creative achievements of a person in the general population (Beaty, Smeekens, Silvia, Hodges, and Kane, 2013; Jauk, Benedek, & Neubauer, 2014). Nevertheless, it is obviously limited as it is a momentary datum, extracted from an artificial situation that might not be motivating and significant, and its measurement takes place under the pressure of a limited amount of time. It would be overly simplistic to accept it as a way to understand the creative potential of a person with ASD, for creativity–as with intelligence–probably expresses itself and walks different paths in the autistic mind. We cannot approach creativity in people with ASD with the same concepts and instruments developed for the general population.

There are many demonstrations that people with ASD can be creative. We only need to observe their creations to convince ourselves of their genuine aesthetic value. For instance, the books *Drawing*

Autism, by Jill Mullin (2009), and *The Art of Autism-Shifting Perceptions*, by Debra Hosseini (2012), are impressive compilations of different works from different autistic artists, many of whom acclaimed by professional critics and internationally famous.

Moreover, recent experimental studies showed surprising results. Kasirer and Mashal (2014), for example, observed that adults with ASD not only performed similarly to those from the control group when interpreting known and new metaphors, but also presented works that are more original. This finding becomes more unexpected if we consider the known difficulties in verbal communication for a person on the spectrum. Another study showed that people with a higher tendency to systematization–a characteristic of ASD–had better performance in tasks of divergent thinking (Takeuchi et al., 2014). Monitoring 312 people, Best, Arora, Porter, and Doherty (2015) also observed that autistic traces (quantified from self-evaluation reports) had a positive relationship to originality in tests of divergent thinking, which is to say, people with more prominent autistic tendencies gave less usual, and thus, more creative answers.

After studying the savant syndrome for about 30 years, researcher Darold A. Treffert, in a review paper published in 2014, withdrew a statement he had made decades earlier about the theme, in which he affirmed that savants' abilities were restricted to replication. He then reported having seen several cases, especially in savant musicians, of temporal evolution of artistic behavior, which starts as reproduction, develops into improvisation, and finally results in the creation of original pieces (Treffert, 2014). We should give this report more attention, for it gives us a direction and an opportunity to observe the long-term creative trajectory of people with ASD, including those who are not savants. It is possible that their acquired creative abilities are evident in a more restricted context–one related to their interest area and one observed after a longer time of practice. The inclination of people with ASD towards behavioral rigidity and sameness, characteristics that restrain everyday creativity (involvement with the small inventions and experimentations of everyday such as hobbies, musical improvisations, culinary creations, etc.), do not prevent their creative potential from expressing itself in the areas to which they are dedicated.

As mentioned above, many characteristics of people with ASD can further an interest in art and creative expression. Particularities of perceptual processing can generate new perspectives. Isolation and difficulties in communication and socialization can all allow a freer process of creative production that is independent of the influence of established concepts. In addition, the tendency of people with ASD to focus on an object or activity may induce exhaustive training, experimentation, and, eventually, unusual works.

For the autistic mind, it may be an advantage that perseverance and dedication are independent from external results, which is to say people with ASD have the capability to give their all to a task, moved by the fascination and pleasure that derive from the activity or object at hand. On the contrary, non-autistic people may base their efforts generally on expected results, and this future expectation is often what

XXIV. Hallows ("Relíquias") 40 cm x 50 cm – acrylic paint, 2015

"...the painting has a life of its own. I try to let it come through". Jackson Pollock

"I thought about the movie *Harry Potter and the Deathly Hallows*." Cacá Silva motivates them. They may evaluate a performance, a product, or an ability by the prestige, profit, or recognition that it brings them. A dance, a song, a painting, a scientific idea, or an invention needs to be exposed and appreciated in order to be relevant to non-autistic people. Even when non-autistic people keep their creations hidden, they picture an audience–even if just vaguely–during the creative process. On the one hand, this characteristic facilitates their social adequacy, for they orientate their effort toward the needs and values of their community. On the other hand, the dependency on the judgment of others may cause a lot of suffering and uncertainty. Moreover, history shows that many geniuses died without knowing their genius and even believed themselves to be failures, such as writer Franz Kafka, poet Fernando Pessoa, and painter Vincent van Gogh, or people like painter Frida Kahlo and philosopher Schopenhauer, who received recognition only in their last years of life. How many findings were never uncovered because scientists, influenced by lack of comprehension and criticism by their peers, doubted their capabilities before finally giving up? It is fascinating to think that someone can be submerged in a universe of his or her own, work unstoppably on a task for months or years, creating freely and without a care for–or without even considering–the reception and the impact of his or her creations.

On the one hand, restricted interests can be highly debilitating, as they consume a great amount of time and mental energy, and do not allow engagement in other occupations. On the other hand, they may constitute a bridge of interaction between the child with ASD and the world. Parents and educators are encouraged nowadays to recognize and share the focus of interest as a start to removing the child from his or her isolation, leading to a more enriching and complex level of involvement that might generate creative works or performances that are worthy of the group, promoting social integration. The American artist, Jessica Hillary Park[10] , is an example. Her parents slowly directed her fascination for geometric forms, colors, heating controllers, radio displays, etc. toward drawing and painting of both buildings and houses. Her art evolved through the years, and freer compositions with greater interest in the global aesthetical effect gradually replaced the systematic and microscopic reproduction of details. Nowadays, she is a renowned painter and is financially independent because of her paintings. She understood that people would be more interested in the portrayal of their own homes or of their town buildings than in portraits of pipes. Her mother, who saw in art a means for social education, describes in two touching books the childhood of her daughter, her struggles, and her evolution: The Siege, the First Eight Years of *an Autistic Child* (Park, 1967) and *Existing Nirvana, a Daughter's Life with Autism* (Park, 2002).

---

[10] Retrieved from http://folkart.org/mag/jessica-park

The normal brain is a myth: Asperger syndrome and neurodiversity

Regardless of being abolished by the current classification of American Psychiatric Association (2013), the term Asperger Syndrome is already firmly established in the mind of the public, including in autism support groups, associations, and virtual communities. The name is a tribute to Austrian physician Hans Asperger who described the syndrome in 1944. The syndrome is defined in particular by the clear preservation of intelligence but with difficulties in socialization and nonverbal communication, as well as repetitive behavior, and restricted interests (American Psychiatric Association, 1994; Casella, Rodrigues, Souza, & Morais, 2013).

For many people, to receive this diagnose after years of suffering is liberating, for it finally explains their behavior and is an assurance that they are not "crazy", "weird", or "stupid". Being an "Aspie" (as many of them call themselves) means not being alone, but belonging to a group, and having an identity that can be presented to society. Gradually, a sense of "Aspie pride" has grown, expressing self-acceptance and a definition of oneself as a person with not only difficulties and limitations, but also potentials. The Asperger community does not discount or minimize the deficits related to ASD. On the contrary, many leaders of these communities offer intimate reports of their lives, their stories, and of the restrictions and challenges they still face. The point is to show society that deficits are only a part of what someone can be, live, and accomplish.

In this context, Neurodiversity began in the United States as a movement within the Autism Rights Movement, asserting that the world needs all kinds of brains and that our historical development as species in fact took place due to the contributions of atypical minds. Their discourse, based on genetic, anthropologic, and evolutionary psychology data, holds that our genomic differences allowed human behavior and skills to be manifested in a wide range of variations and combinations that, despite being seen as disorders, were maintained across the thousands of years of our evolution specifically due to the fact that they do not just encompass difficulties and weakness, but also include aspects positive for the individual and the group (Blume, 1998). For instance, bipolar tendency (affective instability) and schizotypal trait (the tendency to develop eccentric associations) are aspects of personality that may be associated with severe psychiatric disorders, but also with a higher level of creativity. The autism spectrum may reach a severity that incapacitates a person, but it can also contribute to increased development in different areas, such as those that involve systems (e.g., computational language and mathematics), perception of details, memory, long-term focus, and pattern detection. People with dyslexia are an example of another disorder related to positive aspects, as they have a better visual-spatial ability and 3D image thinking (Armstrong, 2015).

XXV. Earth ("Terra")

50 cm x 70 cm – glue and acrylic paint, 2013

"It's not about facts, it's about feelings. It is about remembering feelings and happiness. A definition of art is that it makes concrete our most subtle emotions. I think the highest form of art is music. It's the most abstract of all art expression." Agnes Martin

"It is the Earth, the planet, even if doesn't look like it." Cacá Silva

The words of Temple Grandin (2006) translate spectacularly the idea of Neurodiversity:

> In an ideal world, the scientist should find a method to prevent the most severe forms of autism but allow the milder forms to survive. After all, the really social people did not invent the first stone spear. It was probably invented by an Aspie who chipped away at rocks while the other people socialized around the campfire. Without autism traits, we might still be living in caves.

Thus, the concept of a division of the population between normal and abnormal is excluding and discriminatory, and does not correspond to the neurobiological and evolutionary reality. The normal brain is a myth. The new perspective proposes–instead of disorder, disease, or syndrome–the term *neurodiversity*, which implicates the acknowledgement of weakness, but also of positive qualities.

Participants from the Autism Rights Movement seek to reclaim a better social acceptance, inclusion in the job market, and development of support structures (psychotherapies, social media, and events). They understand that socialization and the overcoming of difficulties must be promoted, however, without obligating them to emulate the behavioral patterns of neurotypical people.

In fact, inclusion is more than just an ethical edict; it is an economic need in society. Considering the prevalence rate of ASD and also of other psychiatric and neurological disorders, people who are not neurotypical account for at least 10% of the general population (Konkiewitz, 2013; Lopes et al., 2016; Polanczyk, Salum, Sugaya, Caye, & Rohde, 2015; Steel et al., 2014). How could we leave all those thousands of people outside of the processes of education, professionalization, and work?

Instead of imagining inflexible parameters of normality as a precondition for social participation (e.g., models of appearance and behavior to be part of a group), it would be more constructive to transform enterprises, schools, and public organizations, for example, into integrational spaces where people were individually analyzed and supported so they could give the best of themselves.

The school as a space for opportunities: integration, bullying, and peer-mediated interventions

Schools urgently need to become true–instead of just alleged–places for opportunity. Students should comprehend diversity from childhood and should be encouraged to cooperate instead of compete (Konkiewitz, 2015a; Ladd, 1990; McConnell, 2002). Students with ASD can overcome obstacles of socialization if they are involved in group activities associated with their personal interests. To share a project with others may be a path not only to develop language, but also to comprehend social rules. Additionally, when a child presents his or her skills, the group will see him or her as more than just weird, an appreciation that will change this child's self-image and the image he or she has of the environment.

It is not difficult to promote cooperative situations. Children and teenagers are flexible and curious. The first step is to put an end to our ancient paradigms. To include is not simply to allow someone different to occupy the same space as others by means of some architectural adaptations. To include is to integrate. An integrative environment needs information, awareness, and the deconstruction of prejudice. Children, parents, and educators must be completely convinced that inclusion will not damage the education of the children, and that the school will truly guarantee the needs of the children. When a child teaches something to another; when a child elaborates a strategy to achieve a goal, searching for information to do so; when a child divides the steps of a task among members of a group, and when the objective is finally achieved, this child develops various life-long cognitive, metacognitive, social, and emotional skills.

One needs to know that everybody has limitations in order to learn to give people respect. We need to put an end to the environment of classrooms in which we select the best student, whom others must mirror. We also need to clarify to the other students the peculiar characteristics of a child with ASD, OCD, Tourette syndrome, epilepsy, or any other particularity so that classmates do not bring false information from home.

For people with ASD, the environment must be predictable and organized. New information is best presented visually, through posters and drawings for example. It is also important to know and respect the increased sensitivity of ASD persons to sound, touch, and light, to understand their need for isolation, their difficulties in expression, and other individual characteristics.

When schools and educators gain knowledge of individuals and their strengths and limitations and through this knowledge, the conviction that we can change things, they can transform the mentalities of families and children, and create a cooperative environment. The children with their formidable minds are more than capable of doing the rest. By learning to live together and to work toward a common goal, children intuitively focus on an object of interest, which becomes an element of both union of the group and self-identification. Fascinated by the elaboration of a tool, a machine, a website, a radio show, a play, or a computer program, children tend to see the best in other people instead of their flaws, which is the usual outcome in a typical competitive environment. There are countless reports of people with ASD who ended their isolation because of shared interests.

Children with ASD have a higher risk of being bullied in school. Physical aggression, intimidation, humiliation, swearing, offensive nicknames, or teasing some example of bullying (Konkiewitz, 2015b; Olweus, 1993).

Bullying can have devastating effects, reducing participation and performance in school, leading to isolation, depression, anxiety, and even self-harm. High-functioning autistic children inserted

XXVI. My Family ("Minha Família") 40 cm x 40 cm – marker pen and acrylic paint, 2010

Art does not reproduce the visible; rather, it makes visible." Paul Klee into a regular education system tend to suffer this type of violence more frequently, as low-functioning autistic people are usually more protected. Thus, if there is only inclusion with no awareness and if no empathy is taught to other children, the results will be the opposite of what was intended.

A study performed in the USA (Zablotsky, Bradshaw, Anderson, & Law, 2014) revealed that 63% of children with ASD had been bullied at least once and 38%, bullied in the prior month. The risk factors were low socioeconomic status, presence of other mental disorders such as ADHD, and difficulty in making new friends.

Another American study (Sterzing, Shattuck, Narendorf, Wagner, & Cooper, 2012) estimated that the national prevalence of victims of bullying among teenagers with ASD was 46.3%. The study showed that teenagers from regular schools who also had ADHD and worse communication skills had a higher risk of being bullied.

Aside from the direct training of socioemotional and communication skills offered by therapists, individually or in a group, there are peer-mediated interventions, which is to say interventions by children of the same age or a little older than the child with ASD. In this case, the interventions may be provided by children with typical development that have special charisma and socialization capability, usually chosen by teachers to be trained to stimulate their colleagues to behave appropriately and to participate in the group. For instance, a neurotypical child can learn how to identify classmates who are socially isolated, have difficulty in interacting and are in need of help for achieving better socialization, without being asked to focus on ASD children. The neurotypical child can then learn how to support these children through direct instructions, by providing examples of standard behavior, role reversal, behavior practice, etc. One advantage of this approach is that it does not single out ASD children and has the potential to benefit all children in the class in need of help with socialization.

A study with sixty elementary school children with ASD compared two types of therapy that lasted six weeks each. Results showed that peer-mediated intervention had better effects than individual training, increasing participation in the group, improving social abilities inside the classroom, and diminishing isolation during games in the park. After three months, a reevaluation showed that these changes were still present (Kasari, Rotheram-Fuller, Locke, & Gulsrud, 2012).

Peer-mediated intervention has the advantage of occurring in the natural space of the child and not in a therapeutic context, which is an artificial and protected place, where the child can learn and train for abilities that may or may not be transferred to everyday situations. Another advantage lies in the fact that the intervention stimulates not only the children with ASD but also their peers, which contributes to improvement of the school environment. In fact, the children chosen as mediators are often popular in class and their mere association with the children with ASD increases the acceptance by other children.

The fear that the mediator children could have any social or emotional loss was not confirmed (Locke, Rotheram-Fuller, & Kasari, 2012). On the contrary, intervention allowed them to improve their empathy, their comprehension of individual differences, and their prosocial behavior without reducing their charisma or the quality of their previous friendships.

Employment as a space of opportunity: all types of thinking can be constructive

Having a job means having a place in society, having an organized routine, interacting with other people outside the family circle, and understanding oneself as someone capable of participating in society and contributing to it. Employment bestows a sense of dignity and purpose, and the financial compensation of a job allows higher independence and freedom of self-determination. Moreover, economic studies demonstrate that investing in inserting people with ASD into the job market bears financial benefits for all of society (Jacob, Scott, M. Falkmer, & Falkmer, 2015; Mavranezouli et al., 2014). Unfortunately, however, the employment rate of people with ASD is very low; in 2015, only 20% had a job, according to the United Nations (Ki-moon, 2015).

In the job market, as in school, specific interests of ASD individuals have to be stimulated and gradually widened and directed to the acquisition of relevant knowledge and to increased professional skills. For instance, visual processing skills may be oriented to technical drawing and computational graphics. In her biography, *The Way I See It*, Temple Grandin (2011) highlights the importance of individualized orientation and supervision in this process and reveals the crucial role that mentors performed in her life, especially her high school teacher, Mr. Carlock, who made her believe in her own ideas and choose her own path. She explains that "Mentors did, indeed, play a pivotal role in helping me become the person and professional I am today. They can be valuable catalysts to helping the spectrum child or teen learn fundamental study and research skills that will propel them to a future career" (Grandin, 2011).

In a more recent book, *Developing Talents: Careers for Individuals with Asperger Syndrome and High Functioning Autism* (Grandin & Duffy, 2004), Temple Grandin has developed a practical guide for parents and educators on how to promote individual talents and to insert a person with ASD in the job market.

The need for too many steps to get a job can be limiting. To choose an employer, to write a curriculum, and to go to the first interview all represent huge challenges. Adaptation to the work routine, to the environment, people, and to rules of behavior and communication, and the necessity of flexibility in new situations, and the need for independent planning of tasks all clash with difficulties in communication, socialization, and with difficulties in adapting, which are all autism characteristics.

It is often necessary to prepare and monitor a person with ASD individually, explaining the rules of group socialization, new perspectives, expectations, and possible reactions of other people. The multimedia

XXVII. Hot Air Balloon ("Balão")

40 cm x 60 cm – acrylic paint, 2012

"This ***balloon*** is such a childlike and a dream-state image! It is a magic hot air balloon made of pieces of dreams, a fairytale in smooth and light colors that invites us to untie the ropes of diligence and simply fly." ECK program JobTIPS[11] offers videos, picture cards, exercises, tests, and other tools to train people in five professional steps: 1) determining professional interests; 2) finding a job; 3) getting a job; 4) keeping a job, and 5) leaving a job. Even better is the possibility of rehearsing typical situations in a protected environment, supervised by a therapist.

On one hand, it is recommended that a person with ASD train in basic social skills, on the other hand, the work environment needs to follow the same recommendations that are given to schools: local characteristics of the workplace–such as light levels, noise and the presence of odors–and the circulation of people need to be considered, since people with ASD may have higher sensitivity to these and other forms of stimulation. The routine of the ASD person has to be stable and predictable, and information must be provided explicitly, including making visual resources available if necessary. The immediate superior has to be accessible and capable of establishing direct communication in the face of problems. People need to be prepared to cooperate, to overcome differences, and to break the standard concept of normality. All forms of thinking can be constructive. Furthermore, some inherent characteristics of ASD are potentially very attractive to the job market. Autistic persons tend to be punctual, disciplined, and diligent; they have excellent memory, can concentrate for a great amount of time, are attentive to details, do not lie, do not get involved in personal matters, and do not get distracted with conversations that are not related to work.

[11] *Retrieved from http://www.Do2Learn.com/JobTIPS*

XXVIII. Hope ("A Esperança")

50 cm x 70 cm – acrylic filler and acrylic paint, 2013

"***Hope*** is an attitude toward uncertainty and angst that makes us persevere. Here, hope is colorful, but mostly red. It has no distinguishable form, but it can remind us of a tropical bird, a kite on the wind… Anyway, it is full of energy and ready to face the dynamism of life and flow with it." ECK

"I was inspired by the *Hunger Games* movie." Cacá Silva

6. Final Thoughts

The inspiration and theme of this book is the art of Camila Falchi, which reveals colorful, rich, and intense emotion in its expressive strength, in opposition to monotony, repetitiveness, and coldness, which are typically expected from a person with ASD. This rupture of stereotypes and stigmas opens the mind to a new perspective about autism that coincides with recent evolution in thinking about persons on the spectrum, whether by the scientific world or by social groups such as Asperger communities. The Empathizing-Systemizing Theory (ES) is an example of this new vision, for it proposes a concept of mental functioning that encompasses not only difficulties, but also talents and potentialities associated with ASD.

Autism involves the most complex functions of the brain, ones that distinguish our extraordinary capacity as humans for creative and productive interaction with the world. Research on autism is now attracting the most capable of investigators and is providing new, rich insights into the most complex and challenging of brain functions, including mechanisms that underlie human consciousness. It has given a new grasp of the molecular, physiological and genetic aspects of the brain that differ in neurotypicals and persons on the spectrum. This knowledge may lead to improved, evidence-based diagnosis and eventually to treatments targeted to the needs of the particular individual. In uncovering the basis for the special neural attributes of autistic individuals, new research has confirmed that each brain is unique. It may also provide the general benefit of a better understanding of emotional perception and how we form productive and rewarding interpersonal relationships. This information is certain to form a bridge between people on the spectrum and neurotypicals, and to provide a wider understanding of how the human brain operates generally and is able to provide the highest biological functions found in all of nature.

Characteristics of autism that were seen as debilitating are currently seen as an open window for development. Therefore, restricted interests can be stimulated and channeled to acquire wider skills. The process of conception and elaboration of a product may be the bridge not only to learning mental strategies such as planning, sequencing, and self-control, but also to communication and socialization.

Art and music therapies, work groups, and orientation with a tutor are examples of paths that can benefit people with ASD by exploring their potentials and leading them to a path of self-discovery and self-organization.

This text has discussed the limitations of procedures and theoretical concepts commonly used to evaluate the intelligence and creativity of people with ASD. It also presented evidence that these capacities of people with ASD are probably underestimated and misunderstood because of these factors. It is clear that the brain is dynamic and can be molded; hence, all inflexible definitions of the potentials of people with ASD are underestimations and are reductionist.

This discussion has direct and wide implications for the educational system, the job market, and for social structure, because the way we see and promote people is the basis for their true integration and contribution to the group. The survival of society, not only in its ethical, but also in its economic aspects, will depend on a change in paradigms that stimulates creative opportunities for different people, and that is capable of enriching itself with the diversity of its members.

We hope that the future can bring us a more complete understanding of autism and of the human mind, and new possibilities to integrate and to support all persons that do not fit into the imagined ideal of normality. Let our world become increasingly free of rigid and exclusionary stigmas, and become a place with many doors so that creativity and life can enter flourish in all of their various shapes.

XXIX. World ("Mundo") 60 cm x 70 cm – acrylic filler over acrylic paint, 2013

"The ***World*** is warm, agitated, intense, and full of emotions: an avalanche, everything at the same time. It is a universe that bubbles, overflows; it is hard to understand. Many times, the mind is overloaded and suffers from anxiety." ECK

"It depends... It reminds me of our imaginary world." Cacá Silva

7. The Words of a Mother

Camila's patron saint is Saint Camillus de Lellis, the patron saint of the sick, hospitals, nurses and physicians. She is my middle child. However, being in the middle was never gratuitous to her. We painted her prelude with violent brushstrokes before she was even born. In the heart of a newborn family–a mother, a father, a three-month old baby, and a small budget–I got pregnant. Initially, I was overwhelmed by the light and happiness of having a second child on the way, but, during the first trimester of pregnancy, I got rubella. Scared, I dreaded the future. I cannot deny that the shadow of abortion stained the following months with doubt.

I chose to continue, in spite of the foreboding words from my colleagues. It was not the easiest decision, it probably is not to any woman, but it was certainly my best choice. Amid many all these bad premonitions, Camila was delivered on March 28, 1991, a Maundy Thursday, at 4:55 PM, in Votuporanga, a small town in Brazil. Regardless of the intrauterine restriction of growth and all the complications that my condition could have caused her, she was born healthy and breathing, measuring 18.8 inches and weighting 101.2 ounces. We left the hospital on Easter Sunday.

Feeling forsaken, I tried to nourish my uncertainties with the strength of medical convictions. At the very beginning, we had a pediatrician who advised me to accept her special condition and to comprehend the limitations expected of her. However, I believed in individual power and even if studies predicted she would be just another point on a curve, I got attached to the idea that she would be the bend of this determinism, a point outside the statistical curve.

I moved mountains, I fell into valleys, I made lakes and rivers out of tears; we crossed barriers. I climbed the shoulders of giants: I searched for great professionals, but, above all, I found great human beings to whom I am still grateful: Dr. Antonio Seba Jr., the pediatrician who accompanied Camila and never gave up so that the flame of health inside her would never extinguish. Dr. Mauro Spinelli, the speech therapist who tenderly treated her language disorder until his premature death. Dr. Hélio Thomaz, the neurologist who never stopped believing in the potential of my daughter, a wise man in his art and an artist in life who told me in a voice full of hope that she "can be whatever she wants, do whatever she wants; don't ever stop believing." I never did. Those are the reasons why I kept going on: speech therapists, occupational therapists, child therapists, psychotherapy, ballet, sports, physiotherapy, psychoanalysis...

The path was again full of obstacles. She did not gain weight; she could not suck during nursing. At six months old, she did not sit down. She did not crawl. She started to walk clumsily at the age of two. She started having absence seizures at a very young age, and had an early autism diagnosis. We won battle after battle, we had to fight hard; we tasted bitterness mixed with disillusions and reality shocks; but we kept moving. Suddenly we had a new problem: she was at the age of going to school. I was unwilling to take her to a special school, although regular ones did not accept her. We adapted our family dynamic; we moved to different cities and changed habits until a regular school accepted her.

I chose the COOPEN school, in São José do Rio Preto, a city not far from where we used to live. When the pedagogical coordinator asked me about my expectations, my answer was very clear to me: "I want her to have learned how to read and write by the time she graduates." Being very attentive, teachers taught her the formal content in nontraditional ways, including movies, which she always loved. With the help of tutors during her classes, we climbed a few more steps in her development. Yet, frustration walked hand in hand with accomplishments. She graduated in high school without knowing how to read or write. We have not given up. Camila longs for the day when she learns to read. It is her biggest dream. She goes to supplementary classes and now she can recognize letters and syllables; she reads, comprehends, and even writes small sentences; she can also solve elementary mathematical operations.

Problems never stopped piling up. We have fought continuous battles since her adolescence against OCD. Fortunately, we now have another warrior fighting for our cause: Camila, who now understands her problems and tries to control herself. Some of them are even humorous, like when she wore her school uniform every day for years and we used to make fun of the situation by saying that she was the best advertisement COOPEN ever had. We adapt ourselves to avoid some forbidden words: "death" became "to kick the bucket"; "panties" became "tananam"; "skewer" became "foodstick", etc.

When she was 18 years old, at the beginning of high school, Camila started to take painting lessons. I confess that my ignorance about art blurred my perception of such potential. However, our warrior played the leading role in her art and made weapons out of brushes and strategy out of sensibility. She

XXX. Imagination ("Imaginação")

50 cm x 70 cm – acrylic paint, 2014

"***Imagination*** – I chose this painting as a present from Cacá Silva when we held her artistic exhibition during the II International Grand Dourados Neuroscience Symposium, in 2014. I see in it a majestic bird, opening its wings to fly. I wish that many others could also see in all people with disabilities, syndromes, or any other allegedly limitation this powerful and revealing image. Indeed, a bird like this lives in each one of us." ECK earned the respect of her painting teacher unaided and threw herself into the world as an artist, profession that now she identifies herself.

The text you now read exists today as a fruition of the endeavor and perception of the great minds that Camila's art has touched. I am especially grateful to Professor Elisabete Castelon Konkiewitz, who has decisively contributed crucially to Camila's appropriation of her own identity as an artist when she invited my daughter to exhibit her paintings during the II International Grand Dourados Neuroscience Symposium, in 2014. Nowadays, Camila wants to one day make a living from painting, while taking care of her pets (two dogs, Brieta and Henry), and to keep living, full of what we can see in her paintings: happiness. Camila is, above all, happy, and this is our greatest victory.

Eliana Falchi Parra Carvalho da Silva,
São José do Rio Preto, March 2016.

XXXI. Brazil ("Brasil")

30 cm x 40 cm – acrylic paint, 2015

"Only our heart can make us better, and that is the main purpose of art." Cândido Portinari

"I intended to show my indignation with everything that has been happening in Brazil, but despite everything it is the best place to live." Cacá Silva

8. References

Alexander, A. L., Lee, J. E., Lazar, M., & Field, A. S. (2007). Diffusion tensor imaging of the brain. *Neurotherapeutics, 4*(3), 316-329.

Allen, R., Hill, E., & Heaton, P. (2009). 'Hath charms to soothe ...': An exploratory study of how high-functioning adults with ASD experience music. *Autism, 13*(1), 21–41.

Ameis, S. H., & Catani, M. (2015). Altered white matter connectivity as a neural substrate for social impairment in Autism Spectrum Disorder. *Cortex, 62*:158-181.

American Psychiatric Association. (1994). *Diagnostic and statistical manual of mental disorders, Fourth Edition*. Washington, DC: American Psychiatric Press.

American Psychiatric Association (2013). *Diagnostic and statistical manual of mental disorders*. Washington, DC: American Psychiatric Association.

Andrade, P. E., & Konkiewitz, E. C. (2011). Brain and the music: a window to the comprehension of the interactive brain functioning. *Ciências & Cognição, 16*(1), 137-164.

Armstrong, T. (2015). The myth of the normal brain: embracing neurodiversity. *AMA Journal of Ethics, 17*(4), 348-352.

Assaf, M., Jagannathan, K., Calhoun, V. D., Miller, L., Stevens, M. C., Sahl, R., ... Pearlson, G. D. (2010). Abnormal functional connectivity of default mode sub-networks in Autism Spectrum Disorder patients. *Neuroimage, 53*(1), 247-256.

Barnard, R. A., Pomaville, M. B., & O'Roak, B. J. (2015). Mutations and modeling of the chromatin remodeler CHD8 define an emerging autism etiology. *Frontiers in Neuroscience, 17*(9). Retrieved from http://dx.doi.org/10.3389/fnins.2015.00477

Baron-Cohen, S., Ashwin, E., Ashwin, C., Tavassoli, T., & Chakrabarti, B. (2009). Talent in autism: Hyper-systemizing, hyper-attention to detail and sensory hypersensitivity. *Philos Trans R Soc Lond B Biol Sci, 364*(1522), 1377-1383.

Baron-Cohen, S., Leslie, A. M., & Frith, U. (1985). Does the autistic child have a "Theory of Mind"? *Cognition, 21*(1), 37-46.

Beaty, R. E., Smeekens, B. A., Silvia, P. J., Hodges, D. A., & Kane, M. J. (2013). A first look at the role of domain-general cognitive and creative abilities in jazz improvisation. *Psychomusicology: Music, Mind, and Brain, 23*, 262–268.

Best, C., Arora, S., Porter, F., & Doherty, M. (2015). The relationship between subthreshold autistic traits, ambiguous figure perception and divergent thinking. *J Autism Dev Disord, 45*(12), 4064-4073.

Blume, H. (1998, September 30). Neurodiversity: On the neurological underpinnings of geekdom. *The Atlantic*. Retrieved from http://www.theatlantic.com/magazine/archive/1998/09/neurodiversity/305909/.

Borgi, M., Loliva, D., Cerino, S., Chiarotti, F., Venerosi, A., Bramini, M., ... Cirulli, F. (2016). Effectiveness of a standardized equine-assisted therapy program for children with Autism Spectrum Disorder. *J Autism Dev Disord, 46*(1), 1-9.

Brans, R. G., Kahn, R. S., Schnack, H. G., van Baal, G. C., Posthuma, D., van Haren, N. E., ... Hulshoff Pol, H. E. (2010). Brain plasticity and intellectual ability are influenced by shared genes. *J Neurosci, 30*(16), 5519-5524.

Buckner, R. L., Andrews-Hanna, J. R., & Schacter, D. L. (2008). The brain's default network: Anatomy, function, and relevance to disease. *Ann N Y Acad Sci, 1124*, 1-38.

Byers, E. S., Nichols, S., & Voyer, S. D. (2013). Challenging stereotypes: sexual functioning of single adults with high functioning Autism Spectrum Disorder. *J Autism* Dev Disord, 43(11), 2617-2627.

Capriola, N. N., Maddox, B. B., & White, S. W. (2016, June 20). No offense intended: Fear of negative evaluation in adolescents and adults with Autism Spectrum Disorder. *J Autism Dev Disord*. Retrieved from http://link.springer.com/article/10.1007%2Fs10803-016-2827-0

Casella, B. C., Rodrigues, C. L., Souza, L. A. S., & Morais, R. M. C. B. (2013). Meu universo particular: Conhecendo a Síndrome de Asperger. In E. C. Konkiewitz (Ed.), *Aprendizagem, comportamento e emoções na infância e adolescência* (pp. 165-177). Dourados, Brazil: UFGD.

Case-Smith, J., Weaver, L. L., & Fristad, M. A. (2015). A systematic review of sensory processing interventions for children with autism spectrum disorders. *Autism, 19*(2),133-148.

Ceci, S. J. (1996). *On intelligence: A bioecological treatise on intellectual development.* Cambridge, MA: Harvard University Press.

Courchesne, E., & Pierce, K. (2005). Why the frontal cortex in autism might be talking only to itself: Local over-connectivity but long-distance disconnection. *Curr Opin Neurobiol, 15*(2), 225-230.

Csíkszentmihályi, M., & Lefevre, J. (1989). Optimal experience in work and leisure. *J. Pers. Soc. Psychol, 56*, 815–822.

Dapretto, M., Davies, M. S., Pfeifer, J. H., Scott, A. A., Sigman, M., Bookheimer, S. Y., & Iacoboni, M. (2006). Understanding emotions in others: mirror neuron dysfunction in children with Autism Spectrum Disorders. *Nat. Neurosci. 9*(1), 28–30.

Dawson, M., Soulières, I., Gernsbacher, M. A., Mottron, L. (2007). The level and nature of autistic intelligence. *Psychol Sci., 18*(8), 657-662.

de la Torre-Ubieta, L., Won, H., Stein, J. L., & Geschwind, D. H. (2016). Advancing the understanding of autism disease mechanisms through genetics. *Nat Med, 22*(4), 345-361.

Dennett, D. C. (1978). Beliefs about beliefs. *Behavioral and Brain Sciences, 1*(4), 568-570.

Dichter, G. S. (2012). Functional magnetic resonance imaging of Autism Spectrum Disorders. *Dialogues Clin Neurosci, 14*(3), 319-351.

Drake, J. E., & Winner, E. (2011). Realistic drawing talent in typical adults is associated with the same kind of local processing bias found in individuals with ASD. *J Autism Dev Disord., 41*(9), 1192-1201.

Duncan, J. (2005). Prefrontal cortex and Spearman's g. In J. Duncan, L.H. Phillips, & P. McLeod (Eds.), *Measuring the mind: Speed, control, and age* (pp. 249–272). Oxford, England: Oxford University Press.

Duncan, J., Seitz, R. J., Kolodny, J., Bor, D., Herzog, H., Ahmed, A., ... Emslie, H. (2000). A neural basis for general intelligence. *Science 289*(5478), 457–460.

Evans, S. L., Dal Monte, O., Noble, P., & Averbeck, B. B. (2014). Intranasal oxytocin effects on social cognition: A critique. *Brain Res, 1580*, 69-77.

Frith, U., & Frith, C. D. (2003). Development and neurophysiology of mentalizing. *Philos Trans R Soc Lond B Biol Sci, 358*(1431), 459-73.

Gardner, H. (1999). *Intelligence reframed: Multiple intelligences for the 21st century*. New York, NY: Basic Books.

Gotham, K., Marvin, A. R., Taylor, J. L., Warren, Z., Anderson, C. M., Law, P. A., ... Lipkin, P. H. (2015). Characterizing the daily life, needs, and priorities of adults with autism spectrum disorder from Interactive Autism Network data. *Autism, 19*(7), 794-804.

Grandin, T. (2006). *Thinking in pictures, expanded edition: My life with autism*. New York, NY: Vintage Books.

Grandin, T. (2011). *The way I see it, revised and expanded 2nd edition: A personal look at autism and Asperger's*. Arlington, TX: Future Horizons.

Grandin, T., & Duffy, K. (2004). *Developing talents: careers for individuals with Asperger syndrome and high functioning autism*. Shawnee Mission, KS: Autism Asperger Publishing Company.

Greenspan, S. I., & Wieder, S. (2006). Engaging autism: Using the floortime approach to help children relate, communicate, and think. Cambridge, MA: Da Capo Lifelong Books.

Happé, F. G. E., & Frith, U. (2006). The weak coherence account: Detail-focused cognitive style in Autism Spectrum Disorders. *J. Autism Dev. Disord.,* 36, 5–25.

Heaton, P. (2009). Assessing musical skills in autistic children who are not savants. *Philos Trans R Soc Lond B Biol Sci., 364*(1522), 1443-1447.

Heaton, P., & Allen, R. (2009). "With concord of sweet sounds ...": New perspectives on the diversity of musical experience in autism and other neurodevelopmental conditions. *Neurosciences and Music III: Disorders and Plasticity, 1169*, 318–325.

Hosseini, D. (2012). *The art of autism: Shifting perceptions*. San Rafael, CA: The Art of Autism.

Insel, T. R. (2010). The challenge of translation in social neuroscience: A review of oxytocin, vasopressin, and affiliative behavior. *Neuron, 65*(6), 768-79.

Jacob, A., Scott, M., Falkmer, M., & Falkmer, T. (2015). The costs and benefits of employing an adult with Autism Spectrum Disorder: A systematic review. *PLoS One, 10*(10). Retrieved from http://journals.plos.org/plosone/article?id=10.1371/journal.pone.0139896

Jauk, E., Benedek, M., & Neubauer, A. C. (2014). The road to creative achievement: a latent variable model of ability and personality predictors. *European Journal of Personality, 28*, 95–105.

Jones, E. J., Gliga, T., Bedford, R., Charman, T., & Johnson, M. H. (2014). Developmental pathways to autism: A review of prospective studies of infants at risk. *Neuroscience and biobehavioral reviews, 39*, 1-33.

Kandalaft, M. R., Didehbani, N., Krawczyk, D. C., Allen, T. T., & Chapman, S. B. (2013). Virtual reality social cognition training for young adults with high-functioning autism. *J Autism* Dev Disord., *43*(1), 34-44.

Kasari, C., Rotheram-Fuller, E., Locke, J., & Gulsrud, A. (2012). Making the connection: Randomized controlled trial of social skills at school for children with Autism Spectrum Disorders. *J Child Psychol Psychiatry, 53*(4), 431-439.

Kasari, C., Kaiser, A., Goods, K., Nietfeld, J., Mathy, P., Landa, R., ... Almirall, D. (2014). Communication interventions for minimally verbal children with autism: A sequential multiple assignment randomized trial. *J Am Acad Child Adolesc Psychiatry, 53*(6), 635-646.

Kasirer, A., & Mashal, N. (2014). Verbal creativity in autism: Comprehension and generation of metaphoric language in high-functioning Autism Spectrum Disorder and typical development. *Front Hum Neurosci., 8*(615). Retrieved from https://www.ncbi.nlm.nih.gov/pmc/articles/PMC4128218/

Kedar, I. (2012). *Ido in Autismland: Climbing out of autism's silent prison.* United States: Sharon Kedar.

Kennedy, D. P., Redcay, E., & Courchesne, E. (2006). Failing to deactivate: Resting functional abnormalities in autism. *Proc Natl Acad Sci U S A, 103*(21), 8275-8280.

Ki-moon, B. (2015, April 2). *Secretary-General's message for 2015*. United Nations. Retrieved from http://www.un.org/en/events/autismday/2015/sgmessage.shtml

Koegel, R. L., Schreibman, L., Good, A., Cerniglia, L., Murphy, C., & Koegel, L. K. (1989). *How to teach pivotal behaviors to children with autism: A training manual.* Santa Barbara, CA: University of California.

Konkiewitz, E. C. (2013). Transtornos de aprendizado e de comportamento na infância: uma visão transdisciplinar. In E. C. Konkiewitz, E. (Ed.), *Aprendizagem, comportamento e emoções na infância e adolescência* (pp.7-15). Dourados, Brazil: UFGD.

Konkiewitz, E. C. (2014). Neurobiologia da Inteligência, um desafio às Neurociências. In E. C. Konkiewitz, & A. R. Virgolim (Eds.), *Altas habilidades/superdotação, inteligência e criatividade* (pp. 65-98). Campinas, Brazil: Papirus.

Konkiewitz, E. C. (2015a). Como o professor pode ajudar. In E. C. Konkiewitz, & M. A. Boarati, *Criança, família e escola: Promovendo o desenvolvimento e a saúde emocional do seu filho* (pp.31-38). São José dos Campos, Brazil: Pulso.

Konkiewitz, E. C. (2015b). Como prevenir o bullying. In E. C. Konkiewitz, & M. A. Boarati, *Criança, família e escola: Promovendo o desenvolvimento e a saúde emocional do seu filho* (pp. 39-42). São José dos Campos, Brazil: Pulso.

Konkiewitz, E. C., & Andrade, P. E. (2012). Psiquiatria da infância e da adolescência: gene, cérebro, ambiente e individualidade. In G. Aranha, & A. Sholl-Franco (Eds.), *Caminhos da neuroeducação* (pp. 129-144). Rio de Janeiro, Brazil: Ciências e Cognição.

Ladd, G. W. (1990). Having friends, keeping friends, making friends, and being liked by peers in the classroom: Predictors of children's early school adjustment? *Child Development, 61*(4), 1081–1100.

Leekam, S. R., Nieto, C., Libby, S. J., Wing, L., & Gould, J. (2007). Describing the sensory abnormalities of children and adults with autism. *Journal of Autism and Developmental Disorders, 37*, 894–910.

Locke, J., Rotheram-Fuller, E., & Kasari, C. (2012). Exploring the social impact of being a typical peer model for included children with Autism Spectrum Disorder. *J Autism Dev Disord., 42*(9), 1895-1905.

Logothetis, N. K., Pauls, J., Augath, M., Trinath, T., & Oeltermann, A. (2001). Neurophysiological investigation of the basis of the fMRI signal. *Nature, 412*(6843), 150-157.

Lopes, C. S., Abreu, G. A., Santos, D. F., Menezes, P. R., Carvalho, K. M., Cunha, C. F., ... Szklo, M. (2016). ERICA: Prevalence of common mental disorders in Brazilian adolescents. *Rev Saúde Pública, 50*(1). Retrieved from http://dx.doi.org/10.1590/S01518-8787.2016050006690

Maroun, M., & Wagner, S. (2016). Oxytocin and memory of emotional stimuli: Some dance to remember, some dance to forget. *Biol Psychiatry, 79*(3), 203-212.

Mavranezouli, I., Megnin-Viggars, O., Cheema, N., Howlin, P., Baron-Cohen, S., & Pilling, S. (2014). The cost-effectiveness of supported employment for adults with autism in the United Kingdom. *Autism, 18*(8), 975-984.

McConnell, S. R. (2002). Interventions to facilitate social interaction for young children with autism: Review of available research and recommendations for educational intervention and future research. *Journal of Autism and Developmental Disorders, 32*(5), 351–372.

Milosavljevic, B., Carter Leno, V., Simonoff, E., Baird, G., Pickles, A., Jones, C. R., ... Happé, F. (2016). Alexithymia in adolescents with Autism Spectrum Disorder: Its relationship to internalizing difficulties, sensory modulation and social cognition. *J Autism Dev Disord, 46*(4), 1354-1367.

Mottron, L., Dawson, M., Soulières, I., Hubert, B., & Burack, J. (2006). Enhanced perceptual functioning in autism: An update, and eight principles of autistic perception. *J Autism Dev Disord, 36*(1), 27-43.

Mullin, J. (2009). *Drawing autism*. New York, NY: Akashic Books.

Munson, J., Dawson, G., Sterling, L., Beauchaine, T., Zhou, A., Kohler, E., ... Abbott, R. (2008). Evidence for latent classes of IQ in young children with Autism Spectrum Disorder. *American Journal on Mental Retardation, 113*(6), 438–452.

National Center on Birth Defects and Developmental Disabilities. (2014). Prevalence of Autism Spectrum Disorder among children aged 8 years – Autism and developmental disabilities monitoring network, 11 sites, United States, 2010. *MMWR Surveill Summ, 63*(2), 1-21.

O'Haire, M. E., McKenzie, S. J., McCune, S., & Slaughter, V. (2014). Effects of classroom animal-assisted activities on social functioning in children with Autism Spectrum Disorder. *J Altern Complement Med, 20*(3), 162-168.

Olesen, P. J., Westerberg, H., & Klingberg, T. (2004). Increased prefrontal and parietal activity after training of working memory. *Nature Neuroscience, 7*(1), 75–79.

Olweus, D. (1993) *Bullying at school: What we know and what we can do*. Oxford, England: Blackwell.

Ornitz, E. M. (1974). The modulation of sensory input and motor output in autistic children. *Journal of Autism and Childhood Schizophrenia* 4(3), 197–215.

Park, C. C. (1967). *The siege, the first eight years of an autistic child.* New York, NY: Back Bay Books.

Park, C. C. (2002). *Exiting nirvana: A daughter's life with autism*. New York, NY: Back Bay Books.

Perner, J., & Wimmer, H. (1988). Misinformation and unexpected change: Testing the development of epistemic-state attribution. *Psychol Res, 50*(3), 191-197.

Phillips, M. L., Drevets, W. C., Rauch, S. L., & Lane, R. (2003). Neurobiology of emotion perception I: The neural basis of normal emotion perception. *Biol Psychiatry, 54*(5), 504-514.

Polanczyk, G. V., Salum, G. A., Sugaya, L. S., Caye, A., & Rohde, L. A. (2015). Annual research review: A meta-analysis of the worldwide prevalence of mental disorders in children and adolescents. *J Child Psychol Psychiatry, 56*(3), 345-365.

Premack, D., & Woodruff, G. (1978). Does the chimpanzee have a theory of mind? *Behavioral and Brain Sciences, 1*(4), 515-526.

Rapin, I., Dunn, M., Allen, D., Stevens, M., & Fein, D. (2009). Subtypes of language disorders in school-age children with autism. *Developmental Neuropsychology, 34*(1), 66–84.

Rieffe, C., Meerum Terwogt, M., & Kotronopoulou, K. (2006). Awareness of single and multiple emotions in high-functioning children with autism. *J. Autism Dev. Disord, 37*(3), 455–465.

Rogers, S. J., & Dawson, G. (2010). *Early Start Denver Model for young children with autism: Promoting language, learning, and engagement*. New York, NY: The Guilford Press.

Ross, E. D. (2010). Cerebral localization of functions and the neurology of language: Fact versus fiction or is it something else? *Neuroscientist, 16*(3), 222-243.

Ryndak, D. L., Downing, J. E., Jacqueline, L. R., & Morrison, A. P. (1995). Parents' perceptions after inclusion of their children with moderate or severe disabilities. *Journal of the Association for Persons with Severe Handicaps, 20*(2), 147–157.

Schaafsma, S. M., Pfaff, D. W., Spunt, R. P., & Adolphs, R. (2015). Deconstructing and reconstructing Theory of Mind. *Trends Cogn Sci, 19*(2), 65-72.

Schreibman, L., & Stahmer, A. C. (2014). A randomized trial comparison of the effects of verbal and pictorial naturalistic communication strategies on spoken language for young children with autism. *J Autism Dev Disord, 44*(5), 1244-1251.

Scholz, J., Klein, M. C., Behrens, T. E. J., & Johansen-Berg, H. (2009). Training induces changes in white-matter architecture. *Nature Neuroscience, 12*(11), 1370–1371.

Schwartzman, J. S. (2015). Transtornos do espectro do autismo. In F. H. Santos, V. M. Andrade, & O. F. A. Bueno (Eds.), *Neuropsicologia Hoje* (pp. 137-144). Porto Alegre, Brazil: Artmed.

Simonoff, E., Pickles, A., Charman, T., Chandler, S., Loucas, T., & Baird, G. (2008). Psychiatric disorders in children with Autism Spectrum Disorders: Prevalence, comorbidity, and associated factors in a population-derived sample. *J Am Acad Child Adolesc Psychiatry 47*(8), 921–929.

Smith, T., & Eikeseth, S. (2011). O. Ivar lovaas: Pioneer of applied behavior analysis and intervention for children with autism. *J Autism Dev Disord, 41*(3), 375-378.

Soulières, I., Dawson, M., Gernsbacher, M. A., & Mottron, L. (2011). The level and nature of autistic intelligence II: What about Asperger syndrome? *PLoS One, 6*(9). Retrieved from http://journals.plos.org/plosone/article?id=10.1371/journal.pone.0025372

Staub, D., Schwartz, I. S., Galluci, C., & Peck, C. (1994). Four portraits of friendship at an inclusive school. *Journal of the Association for Persons with Severe Handicaps, 19*(4), 314–325.

Steel, Z., Marnane, C., Iranpour, C., Chey, T., Jackson, J. W., Patel, V., & Silove, D. (2014). The global prevalence of common mental disorders: A systematic review and meta-analysis 1980-2013. *Int J Epidemiol, 43*(2), 476-493.

Sternberg, R. J. (1985). *Beyond IQ: A triarchic theory of human intelligence*. New York, NY: Cambridge University Press.

Sterzing, P. R., Shattuck, P. T., Narendorf, S. C., Wagner, M., & Cooper, B. P. (2012). Bullying involvement and Autism Spectrum Disorders: Prevalence and correlates of bullying involvement among adolescents with an Autism Spectrum Disorder. *Arch Pediatr Adolesc Med, 166*(11), 1058-1064.

Stigler, K. A., McDonald, B. C., Anand, A., Saykin, A. J., & McDougle, C. J. (2011). Structural and functional magnetic resonance imaging of Autism Spectrum Disorders. *Brain Research, 1380*, 146-161.

Tager-Flusberg, H., Paul, R., & Lord, C. E. (2005). Language and communication in autism. In F. Volkmar, R. Paul, A. Klin, & D. J. Cohen (Eds.), *Handbook of autism and pervasive developmental disorder* (pp. 335-364). New York, NY: Wiley.

Takeuchi, H., Taki, Y., Sekiguchi, A., Nouchi, R., Kotozaki, Y., Nakagawa, S., ... Hashizume, H. (2014). Creativity measured by divergent thinking is associated with two axes of autistic characteristics. *Front Psychol,* 921. Retrieved from http://journal.frontiersin.org/article/10.3389/fpsyg.2014.00921/full

Travers, B. G., Adluru, N., Ennis, C., Tromp, P. M., Destiche, D., Doran, S., ... Alexander, A. L. (2012). Diffusion tensor imaging in Autism Spectrum Disorder: A review. *Autism Res, 5*(5), 289-313.

Treffert, D. A. (2009). The savant syndrome: An extraordinary condition. A synopsis: Past, present, future. *Philos Trans R Soc Lond B Biol Sci, 364*(1522), 1351–1357.

Treffert, D. A. (2014). Savant syndrome: Realities, myths and misconceptions. *J Autism Dev Disord, 44*(3), 564-571.

Treffert, D. A., & Rebedew, D. L. (2015). The savant syndrome registry: A preliminary report. *WMJ, 114*(4), 158-162.

Van Steensel, F. J. A., Bögels, S. M., & Perrin, S. (2011). Anxiety disorders in children and adolescents with Autistic Spectrum Disorders: A meta-analysis. *Clin Child Fam Psychol Rev, 14*(3), 302-317.

Wan, C. Y., Demaine, K., Zipse, L., Norton, A., & Schlaug, G. (2010). From music making to speaking: Engaging the mirror neuron system in autism. *Brain Res Bull, 82*(3-4), 161-168.

Weitlauf, A. S., McPheeters, M. L., Peters, B., Sathe, N., Travis, R., Aiello, R., ... Warren, Z. (2014). *Therapies for children with Autism Spectrum Disorder: Behavioral interventions update* (Report No 14-EHC036-EF). Rockville, MD: Agency for Healthcare Research and Quality.

Wimmer, H., & Perner, J. (1983). Beliefs about beliefs: Representation and constraining function of wrong beliefs in young children's understanding of deception. *Cognition, 13*(1), 103-128.

Wood, A., Rychlowska, M., Korb, S., & Niedenthal, P. (2016). Fashioning the face: Sensorimotor simulation contributes to facial expression recognition. *Trends Cogn Sci, 20*(3), 227-240.

Wood, J. J., Drahota, A., Sze, K., Har, K., Chiu, A., & Langer, D. A. (2009). Cognitive behavioral therapy for anxiety in children with Autism Spectrum Disorders: A randomized, controlled trial. *Journal of Child Psychology & Psychiatry, 50*(3), 224–234.

Zablotsky, B., Bradshaw, C. P., Anderson, C. M., & Law, P. (2014). Risk factors for bullying among children with Autism Spectrum Disorders. *Autism, 18*(4), 419-427.

Ziats, M. N., & Rennert, O. M. (2016). The evolving diagnostic and genetic landscapes of Autism Spectrum Disorder. *Front Genet,* 65. Retrieved from http://journal.frontiersin.org/article/10.3389/fgene.2016.00065/full.

Made in the USA
Monee, IL
12 November 2026

67388636R00059